MW00720066

IS THIS
ALL
THERE
IS?

IS THIS ALL THERE IS?

A STORY ABOUT DISCOVERING
YOUR GREATEST POSSIBILITIES

ANDREAS ABELE

ABC PUBLISHING COMPANY
VANCOUVER, BRITISH COLUMBIA

IS THIS ALL THERE IS?

© 2005 by Andreas Abele

Published by:
ABC Publishing Company, Vancouver, Canada
info@abcpublishing.ca
www.abcpublishing.ca

First Edition
Printed in China
Art Direction: Natasha Zippan

The events and characters in this story are purely fictional and any resemblance they may have to any person living or dead is merely coincidental.

Library and Archives Canada Cataloguing in Publication
Abele, Andreas, 1969-
    Is this all there is? : a story about discovering your greatest possibilities / Andreas Abele.

ISBN 0-9738186-0-3

1. Self-actualization (Psychology). I. Title.
  BF637.S4A345 2005   158.1   C2005-904014-9

In loving memory of Maurice Patton

CONTENTS

IS THIS ALL THERE IS?

Have you ever wondered what your greatest possibilities are? Have you ever wished for a map to guide you through the initial steps of exploring what is possible for you? *Is this all there is?* provides you with an entertaining guide through the Five Power Steps, a highly effective process for discovering new and exciting possibilities in your life. As you follow the story of Sam, Ron, and Lynn and witness the two old friends and their new-found acquaintance embark on a journey in search of greater fulfillment and happiness, you will learn how to take advantage of discontent to discover your greatest possibilities.

The Five Power Steps process has been developed over a decade of research and application in business, organizational, and personal transitions, and the principles have been applied with great success in hundreds of mentoring sessions and seminars with executives, leaders, and many other people from all walks of life. Each of the five chapters in this book is devoted to illustrating one Power Step through the experiences of the characters. Each step is summarized at the end of the chapter, along with exercises meant to challenge and support you in your own change process.

Many people and organizations have benefited from the principles outlined in this book. Perhaps the experiences of Sam, Ron, and Lynn will inspire and encourage you to explore what is possible in your own situation as well. Discontent is rarely fun and changes are never easy. But as you will discover, they hold the key to your greatest possibilities.

THE FIVE
POWER STEPS

THE FIRST POWER STEP:
Explore the Power of Your Discontent

THE SECOND POWER STEP:
Face the Power of the Unknown

THE THIRD POWER STEP:
Discover the Power of Your Potential

THE FOURTH POWER STEP:
Take Effective Action to
Realize Your Potential

THE FIFTH POWER STEP:
Receive the Results and
Enjoy Your Successes

ONE

THE FIRST POWER STEP:
Explore the Power of Your Discontent

"Ron, my friend, how are you? It's Sam."

It took me a second to connect the name with the familiar voice on the other end of the phone. "Sam?" I replied in surprise. "Sam Renton? I haven't talked to you in ages!"

I was on my way to the airport, about to head out on another business trip. In fact, it was the third trip in as many weeks. As a consultant for a business group, traveling to clients' locations had been my life for a while now. I was about to ask how he was doing when he got right to the point of his call. His voice became serious.

"Listen Ron, I could use your help on something. Is there any way we can get together for a cup of coffee? I would really appreciate it. There are a couple of things I need to talk to you about."

Sam and I knew each other from way back. We had graduated from the same college more than ten years ago, and I realized with a start that it had been nearly this long since I'd spoken to him. So much had happened since, so much had changed. We had set out together then, Sam and I, to make lives for ourselves. Right after graduation Sam had started a sporting goods store and I had pursued a consulting career with dreams of great success. But I had lost touch with Sam shortly after he had gotten married.

Over the years I had followed Sam's life from a distance. His reputation as a successful entrepreneur grew as he added a second store, and then another, until he had developed a major chain of sporting goods outlets throughout the region. The last time I had heard of Sam was when a local business newspaper recently profiled his company as one of the success stories in town.

I was curious, and more than happy to meet with Sam. I assumed he needed advice about the business expansion plans that had been mentioned in the article I'd seen, advice I would be more than happy and qualified to give. My consulting office and the head office of Sam's chain were both located downtown, and I knew of a great place where we could meet.

"Sure Sam, no problem. Do you know Lynn's, at the far end of downtown?" I asked.

Lynn's Diner was a quiet little place that I liked to visit from time to time when I needed to think. It was unpretentious and simple, and there was a calm feeling of home about the diner.

"Sure I do," he replied. "Cozy little spot. Excuse me, Ron, hold on a second."

In the background, I could hear him speak to what seemed to be one of his employees. "Are these the financials, Robin? You realize they were due Friday, don't you? Everyone is waiting for them. These need to be distributed immediately!"

He barked further directions before returning to the receiver. "Listen Ron, I've got to run here, but can I see you at Lynn's sometime next week? How is Thursday for lunch? Let's say noon?"

I was excited at the prospect of this unexpected reunion and was looking forward to hearing all about the successes and accomplishments I had read about in the paper. As far as I had seen, Sam had reached for the stars and had actually gotten ahold of some.

"I'm back in town by then, so that would be great," I agreed.

"Thanks, Ron," said Sam, and he hung up the phone. I had no idea then about the life-changing events that this simple phone call would trigger. I was expecting to reconnect with an old friend and give him some advice on how to manage the changes that his rapidly growing business was going through. As it turned out, there was a lot more to be discovered than I could have expected. I had been a change management consultant for nearly ten years now, but I had no idea of the biggest change life had in store for me.

✳ ✳ ✳

Throughout my trip, I looked forward to meeting with Sam the following week. On the plane home I thought back to our college days and to the time when Sam had started his first store. I remembered helping him put up store shelving the weekend before his grand opening. The prospect of reuniting with Sam reminded me of what life had been about in those days, when anything seemed possible.

As far as I was concerned, Sam had the perfect life. He had become one of the more prominent business figures in our area and I suspected that he now had more than enough money to retire if he wanted. That alone was an impressive accomplishment, but I'd never been sure if Sam was more fortunate because of his quick rise to success, or because of the partner he had found for life. I remembered the months after Sam had started his first store and how he had proposed to his college sweetheart, Mary-Jane, a college friend of mine as well. They had gotten married the following year. But soon after their wedding, my career had begun to take off and the never-ending stream of business trips had started. It was not too long before my friendships began to dry up.

I thought back to his and Mary-Jane's wedding. It had been a wonderful occasion, and an even better party. Their tenth wedding anniversary had to be fast approaching. I was sure that Mary-Jane's life had not stood still either. The last I'd heard, she was an editor for the arts and lifestyle section of the local daily.

Frankly, Sam's success had always made me a bit envious. Not that I hadn't been successful. I had even made partner at my firm. But my career was also wearing on me. Living out of a suitcase most of the year had not helped me to create a stable life. I had seen a lot of the world, but my few attempts at relationships had failed miserably due to my inability to stick around, in the most literal sense of the word. Lately, I had been thinking a lot about what might have happened had I chosen a different career. Would I be happier?

I was excited when the day of the meeting finally rolled around, and I arrived at Lynn's Diner a little early in anticipation. As I waited for Sam, my thoughts returned to the accomplishments and stature my friend had achieved since we'd graduated. He was an impressive man, and I was nervous that my own life wouldn't measure up to the stories he would have to share.

I imagined what he would look like after all these years: energetic and successful, no doubt. But when Sam opened the door at last, I was surprised. Instead of the vital man I had envisioned, Sam looked tired and his wrinkled shirt and pants were not those of the powerful businessman I had anticipated. I had known Sam to be a little loud and overly confident at times, but he had obviously not come to boast that day. After a quick exchange of hellos, he slid into the booth with a sigh.

"Thanks for coming, Ron. I felt a little strange asking you to meet with me after all these years, but, to be honest, I just didn't know who else to call. I need to talk to someone whose opinion I trust, and I always felt we could talk, you know, about anything. I always thought you had a knack for understanding problems. I mean, it is what you've gone on to do professionally."

It was true. My job consisted of unraveling business problems and advising companies on how to resolve them successfully. Change management was an interesting career and, despite my qualms about my job, I had always enjoyed the topic. I started to gear up to discuss Sam's business problems when he proceeded to explain why he had called me.

"Listen, thanks for meeting up with me here. I thought that maybe you could help me. You see, the thing is…" He hesitated. "The thing is, I have a pretty good life. I have achieved more than I could have ever imagined, and by all measures my life has been a success. But when it comes right down to it, things just aren't going very well. In fact, I've been feeling down for a while now. I'm just not happy and I can't seem to find my way back to my usual self."

He looked at me with a slightly embarrassed smile. I was confused; I had certainly not expected this. Sam's life had

"discontent": n. lack of contentment, as with one's lot in life (Collin's, 115). "dissatisfied" (Webster's, 52).
adj.

IS THIS ALL THERE IS?

always seemed charmed. For so many years, his friends—including me—thought he had it made. Sam had always had an endless amount of energy, had always been working on some project or another, had always been boisterous and friendly. Yet here he was, telling me he was unhappy.

As Sam continued to talk that day, I heard about a different Sam than the one I'd remembered. He told me he had been tired for a while, that he had a hard time getting up in the morning and an even harder time getting to sleep at night. He had been getting frustrated too easily with his staff at work and he was definitely frustrated with himself that he couldn't get out of this rut. He was feeling irritated and unhappy with his life. The more he talked the more it became clear to me that even though he had everything that many others aspired to have, it didn't seem to matter. His life had become tainted by a constant feeling of discontent, and it was upsetting him.

Sam talked on for a long time. We finished our lunch and had just been served coffee when he began to talk about Mary-Jane.

"And you know the worst of it all…" He sighed before continuing. "The worst of it is that Mary-Jane and I are struggling as well. Some weeks it seems that my relationship consists mostly of nagging and criticism. Sometimes I feel like I no longer know why I married Mary-Jane. And she's not satisfied either. It's like she doesn't remember who I am or what I'm all about. Everything she used to appreciate about me, well, now it seems to get on her nerves. I just don't know what to do anymore. We have everything we ever wanted, yet our life together is falling apart at the seams."

I could imagine what Mary-Jane must be going through. She had married an overachiever. She had married a guy who had swept her off her feet with his fun-loving nature, irresistible charm, and boundless pool of energy. But the Sam in front of me was not that guy, and I wasn't surprised to hear that their relationship was going through a difficult time.

As I listened to Sam unburden himself, I couldn't help but think that, even in the smooth surface of a picture-perfect life, there are cracks to be found. I was still a little envious—Sam was dealing with cracks in the surface of his life, whereas most of us have to deal with full-blown holes and craters—but Sam's unhappiness was real and it was causing him serious trouble.

Sam's story caught me off guard. I had expected to provide my expertise on how to manage a business through a change process, not help a friend with his discontent. I had no experience helping people address personal problems. In fact, I had always believed that getting out of a rut was something a person had to do on his own; it was not something that could be outsourced.

Nevertheless, I also knew that a good friend was sometimes needed to lend an ear, some advice, and a helping hand. I had always cared about Sam and I was not about to let him down when he needed me most.

As I listened to Sam, it occurred to me that perhaps his problems were similar to the problems of some of the business clients I had encountered over the years. Earlier in my career, I had come across the idea that the problems businesses face are not just problems, but potential opportunities. I had experienced this to be true in many of the change situations I had managed, and I began to think that perhaps the cracks in Sam's life could signify opportunities for change as well. I decided to take a risk.

"Sam," I started, "I'm sorry you're going through a tough time. I mean, it sounds just awful. All these years of effort, only to come to this point."

Sam nodded gravely.

I continued. "To be truthful, this isn't really my area of expertise. I have never really helped anyone with a major personal problem before. But, after putting in my time as a consultant, I have learned that every problem can be an opportunity. I think there might be another way to look at this."

Sam perked up slightly at this thought. "That would be nice, but I have a feeling that's easier said than done." The tension on Sam's face relaxed a bit, but I could see that he was struggling. His unhappiness wasn't a small and passing emotion. It had begun to be a real stumbling block to moving his life forward and enjoying what he had accomplished. To believe that something positive might be found amidst the rubble of discontent could stretch anyone's imagination.

I was about to start explaining my idea when I glimpsed the Sam I had known years ago. Within a split second, he changed the course of our discussion and, ultimately, the course of my life.

"What about you, Ron? Is your life all that you want it to be?"

Sam may have been in a slump, but he was not slow. Somehow, he had sensed my own dissatisfaction with life. I had not accomplished all I wanted. In fact, when it came right down to it, I felt similar to the way Sam said he felt: I was not happy.

I smiled back at him with the same sense of embarrassment he had brought to the table when he first arrived. "You're right, Sam. I guess there are a couple of things about my life that I'm not happy with either." I had to smile.

Although the thought of facing my discontent was disconcerting, there was something humorous about the realization that I had been paid to help companies solve problems for years without applying the same solutions in my life. As I mulled over this irony, Sam looked down at his watch and made up his mind.

"Listen Ron, it's been good to talk with you. And I really appreciate you taking the time, but I've got some meetings to attend this afternoon that I can't miss. It sounds to me that I'm not the only one who could benefit from talking about all this. What if we meet up a few more times, right here at Lynn's? We can explore a bit more and who knows where it could lead. I have a feeling that good things could come out of it. And it's nice to have someone you trust to talk these things over with." He looked at me expectantly.

Something about our conversation seemed to have given Sam a new sense of hope. "So what do you say?" he prodded, looking at me as though there was only one obvious choice.

I felt excited about the thought of continuing our conversation. "I'm in. It seems like we both have enough to talk about for a few more lunches!"

Sam looked relieved and we laughed. The deal was sealed: we would meet at Lynn's Diner once a week for the next while to see if we could find a way to figure out what was making us unhappy.

＊ ＊ ＊

Our next meeting date arrived quickly. I had continued to think about the function of discontent in the days following our first meeting, and had come up with some ideas to discuss with Sam. We had barely sat down and ordered our coffees when I started in on the opening speech I had prepared. I had been gripped by this idea of looking at discontent as a positive force and I wasn't about to waste any time with small talk.

"So I've been thinking about what we talked about last week; you know, that maybe opportunities are hidden somewhere in our problems," I started. "Maybe our feelings of discontent can help us figure out what our next steps should be."

"What do you mean?" Sam asked.

"Well," I responded after a brief moment of reflection, "I mean, how does one solve a problem? I don't know about you, but for me this feeling of unhappiness seems to have been brewing for a while and I haven't come up with a quick fix for it yet. Do you simply come up with an idea for how to do something differently? I don't think so; at least this is not what I have seen in most of the consulting cases I've experienced. Most of the time, change starts with some sort of conflict, or sometimes even a crisis. Either way, it's not pretty."

"I guess that's true," Sam nodded.

Encouraged, I continued. "So I was thinking that our unhappiness might be like a signpost. This discontent could be pointing us in the direction in which our lives need to— or in which we want them to—change. Maybe it's not such a bad thing after all. Maybe it's more like a motivator or a helper—you know, something to get us to notice areas in our lives that need to be addressed."

Sam didn't appear to share my excitement about these ideas. He quietly stirred his pre-lunch coffee with a spoon and grumbled. "Let's suppose you're right. Let's suppose I've been feeling lousy and down and slow and tired because there is some great opportunity lying ahead." Sam's sarcasm was thick. "Why wouldn't I just go out there and take advantage of the opportunity directly? Why would I need to feel lousy first?"

He shook his head and continued.

"It's nice to think that there is some meaning behind this feeling, but it doesn't make sense to me. It's not necessary to feel discontent to be able

POWER STEP ONE
Explore the Power of Your Discontent

FIVE POWER STEPS TIP

Experiencing discontent is not necessarily a negative thing. While it's not pleasant, it is actually one of the most important starting points for discovering what is really possible in your situation. Exploring your discontent allows you to figure out what needs to change in your life. Don't fear discontent. It is actually a signpost pointing you in the direction of your greatest possibilities.

to make a change. I can make a change anytime I want. I can make a change because I have a good idea. I don't need discontent to point me anywhere. I can make up my own mind about what needs to change."

Sam hadn't achieved his success by accident. He was a smart man and the points he made carried weight. But I was committed to exploring the possibilities, and I wouldn't be so easily stopped in my tracks. I didn't have an answer to his challenges, but fumbled my way ahead nonetheless.

"Okay, it's true; you can change anything you want, anytime—or at least you can try. So why do so many people struggle with solving their problems? Why is it hard to make changes even once you've decided to do so?"

Sam looked at me with a question in his face.

"Hmm. Good point. If I wanted to make a change in my life, I could. So why haven't I?"

"Yes," I replied. "Why haven't you, and why haven't I?"

"The only reason I can think of," continued Sam, "is perhaps—"

"—perhaps we don't know what change to make?"

"Exactly."

I was reminded of a particular business case in which a company had practically been forced to discover a new product to survive a period of economic downturn. The product had turned out to be the most successful of their entire line. I charged ahead.

"Maybe our dissatisfaction is indicating opportunities beyond what we would normally consider to be possible in our lives. I remember once when I was young and my dad lost his job for a while. He was really upset. He must have looked for work for a year. But in the end, he found a new career that he loved. Losing his job turned out to be a life-saver. Although he had no idea about the positive results that would come from his search, or even if there would be positive results, life forced him to step beyond what he knew and invited him to discover something different. Maybe it's the same for us. Maybe there are some changes waiting for us, but we can't see what they are right now."

Sam began to nod, his expression indicating increasing clarity about the concept I was promoting.

"So you're saying that discontent comes in when there is an opportunity at hand that isn't part of a person's usual frame of reference, and that perhaps we can use discontent to guide us to changes that we would not be able to see otherwise—bigger picture changes."

There was another minute of silence as Sam continued to stir his coffee. Finally, he nodded. "Maybe you have a point," he said.

We had discovered an interesting aspect of our experience. Our meeting that day lasted well beyond lunch as we talked about our theory and all the things in our lives we were dissatisfied with. Instead of battling our discontent, we could use its powers to propel us ahead and discover new possibilities. In fact, admitting our unhappiness and understanding what it was really about now seemed like the first and most important step in ultimately resolving it. At last, my cell phone rang; it was my assistant calling to alert me to a meeting change. It was time to go.

"I'll see you next week," I said to Sam as I exited the booth. "Same time, same place?" I was beginning to realize how good it felt just to admit my unhappiness. It was a powerful relief to share my thoughts and feelings with someone who shared the same experience and cared about my situation.

"Same time, same place it is," nodded

POWER STEP ONE
Explore the Power of Your Discontent

FIVE POWER STEPS TIP

Once you make peace with the fact that discontent is not a bad thing, you can begin to use it as a tool. Not only does it help you identify areas in your situation that need to change, it also provides you with motivation to move ahead. After all, if you chose not to feel your unhappiness there would be no reason to make a change. A feeling of discontent is an indicator that an opportunity for positive change is at hand. You can use the power of this discontent to propel you ahead in an exploration of your potential.

Sam, and we parted with hopeful feelings that something new and exciting awaited us beyond the frustrations of our current state of mind.

* * *

At our next meeting, Sam shared more stories about the difficulties he had encountered over the past few years. I was amazed; here I had thought he had the perfect life, when really it was as much of a struggle as anyone else's.

We ordered our lunches and continued to talk about the idea of discontent as a signpost that could guide us to discover something new. On this, we clearly agreed. But we still had no idea what to do with all the discontent we had accumulated over the years. It seemed like we had reached another roadblock, and I wondered if we needed some help to overcome it.

We were deep in thought when Lynn—the friendly proprietor of our chosen meeting spot—arrived with our lunches.

"Hi there, boys. How are things?" she asked.

"Not bad, not bad," I replied for the both of us. Lynn wandered to the next table and we continued our discussion. I had noticed Lynn looking over to our booth several times during our meeting the week before, apparently intrigued by the intensity of our extended lunches. This day, however, curiosity seemed to get the better of her; a few minutes later she returned to our table.

"So what are you two discussing, anyhow? It's like you guys hardly touch your food you're so busy talking." She pointed to our plates with a feigned gesture of accusation.

I don't think Sam had been down to Lynn's Diner often, but I was used to her informal ways. She was a dynamic young woman who had run and, as far as I knew, owned the diner for the past number of years. Lynn was the kind of no-nonsense person that made it difficult not to like her, and the diner had become a neighborhood favorite not least because of her way with people and with words.

"Well," muttered Sam, "I suppose we're talking about how to get out of a rut."

"Aren't we all?" Lynn said with a smile, and walked away. It was a brief interlude, and we would never find out just what she was thinking at that moment. Her smile gave me the feeling that she had something to share with us; I momentarily thought about calling her back to our table, but I shrugged off the impulse and Sam and I continued our conversation.

"So how do we figure out the next step?" asked Sam. "How do we go on to beat our unhappiness and figure out the changes we need to make?"

It was the question of the day. As he said it, I had an idea.

"Well, we agree that discontent has the potential to direct us to important changes we can make in our lives. Wouldn't it make sense to take a closer look at our discontent and explore what is really happening? It may sound funny, but the way I look at it, the first step to discover something new and important may be to stop."

Sam looked at me with a raised eyebrow and he shrugged his shoulders. "What do you mean by stopping?" he challenged.

"Well, I feel a bit better already just talking about all this. Maybe we should take the time to experience and understand our discontent further. I don't mean we need to take a vacation or go on a retreat or anything like that. In fact, maybe we have already started to stop. We're already

When I stop and really look at my discontentment what do I see? Why am I dissatisfied with my lot in life? What do I need to do change that? How can I feel better about myself? My lot in life? My relationships? Where I'm at in life?

taking time to think about and talk about and experience our discontent. It seems to be helping, doesn't it?"

Sam was beginning to look more interested. "Yeah, I can see your point there," he replied. "As we've been talking about our unhappiness, we have been learning a lot of new things."

I nodded in agreement. "I don't know about you," I commented, "but I'm

POWER STEP ONE
Explore the Power of Your Discontent

Ironically, one of the first steps in exploring the power of your discontent is to stop and evaluate your feelings. If you are experiencing discontent, take enough time to explore what is really going on in your situation. Seize the opportunity to stop and explore your discontent to discover your most important thoughts. It is in this process of listening to yourself that you can find the strength, courage, and direction to move ahead.

realizing how busy I normally am. I think by stopping and looking at our discontent, it's like I can see how much effort, struggle, and worry is often involved in leading my life. Just thinking about it makes me feel tired. And what kind of stress are we placing on ourselves? That just can't be healthy!"

We laughed and Sam was nodding as we got serious again. It was easy to see the undercurrent of tiredness in his life, and he must have been thinking the same thing when he was looking at me.

"When I stop for a minute and look at my discontent, I really notice something about my relationships as well," he said. "It's like real connections with people elude me in the

Often when I am with other people or in a crowd I feel all alone. How often do I let myself experience a moment deeply enough to truly appreciate?

EXPLORE THE POWER OF YOUR DISCONTENT

rush of my life. I think that's part of what's been happening with Mary-Jane and me."

Sam's comments struck a painful cord with me; I was with people all day but still felt alone in my life.

"Yeah," I nodded. "How often do we let ourselves experience a moment deeply enough to enjoy it? How often do we stop the motion of running our lives to see what comes out of them?"

Sam pondered what I had just said. I added one more thought. "I think once we get a little practice at stopping, we may discover experiences we have been unaware of."

The clinking of coffee spoons was audible in the quiet diner. As I stopped for a minute my mind wandered to my work over the past few years and my life as it stood that day. I felt tired and a wave of feelings arose within me. Sam had been right to challenge me that first day. It was becoming more and more clear to me that I needed these meetings as much as Sam did. Without intending to, I suddenly found myself explaining my own discontent.

"I just don't like my work anymore, Sam," I said with the same sullen face that Sam had brought to our first meeting two weeks earlier. "There was a time when I thought consulting was exciting and a big adventure. When I was made partner at my firm, I felt a sense of accomplishment and success as a result of all the experience I'd gained in my chosen field. But when I really focus on how I feel when I am at work, what I see isn't pretty."

"What do you mean?" asked Sam, looking astounded. "I thought you were pretty good at what you do. I thought you liked it."

"Well…" I started to reply, then paused. Admitting that my career success was not all it appeared to be was not easy. A couple of breaths later, I started again.

"Lately, I can hardly wait until the day is over. I thought it might just be a phase, that maybe I just don't enjoy my job as much as before. But, when I really look at it, I know my feelings are much stronger than that.

"My real feelings are that I do not like my job or my work anymore—and have not for some time." Discontent had secretly gotten the best of me, but I had not fully understood to what extent until that moment.

As I talked about my discontent, I noticed that something seemed to change for Sam as well. He thought and nodded and thought some more. It was as though he was comparing his experience to mine, drawing parallels, and discovering common ground.

"You know," he replied after listening to me, "my life has been a typhoon these past few years. I think I have to take a break from trying to build and build and build." Sam stirred his coffee. "I need to make a change."

Glumly, we looked at each other. There we were: two long lost friends having coffee at a diner, before us the challenge of sorting through what we had accomplished over the past decade, what needed to be discarded, and what needed to be discovered. It seemed like an utterly overwhelming task. So much of who we were was wrapped up in our careers. Education, work experience, risks, challenges, endless amounts of problems, and many successes had shaped our views of who we were. I suddenly had the feeling that we were not only challenging our careers; it seemed as though we were challenging our whole lives.

As we lingered in the diner that day, I realized that by the time Sam and I were honest about our discontent, what it might relate to, and how much it was impacting our lives, we were each facing an escalated set of problems.

Most people are probably familiar with escalating problems. If you don't pay attention to a leaky faucet, you may soon face a puddle on the floor. If you don't clean up the puddle, your kitchen linoleum may warp, and so on. Problems that remain unaddressed have the possibility to escalate. By the time Sam and I began to meet at Lynn's Diner, Sam's marriage was on the verge of collapse and he was in a rut about his business. My attitude toward my job was starting to cost me opportunities with clients, and my colleagues had undoubtedly started to wonder if I was cut out to be a partner in the firm.

I looked over at Sam. I was facing problems, but he was nearly facing a crisis. It seemed the longer discontent was ignored, the higher the stakes. I thought about Sam and Mary-Jane and their lives together. I shuddered to think that their marriage might be destroyed if something didn't change.

I wondered what might have happened if we had each looked at our dissatisfaction

POWER STEP ONE
Explore the Power of Your Discontent

FIVE POWER STEPS TIP

If you ignore discontent, the situation tends to escalate. Opportunities turn into problems, problems into conflicts, conflicts into crises, and crises into destruction, until at last a change is made. But you can de-escalate a situation by taking the time to examine your discontent. Ignoring discontent delays positive change. Exploring discontent becomes a powerful invitation to discover an opportunity for positive change.

in this new way when it had first arisen. Would we have had to face this period of struggle? Or, recognizing the discontent as a signpost, could we have initiated a much more positive, and maybe even enjoyable, process of change?

"So where do we go from here?"

Sam's question jerked me out of my thoughts. The way I saw it now, Sam and I had only two options: continue to ignore our discontent the way we had been, or continue to explore it. Ignoring discontent was not a recipe for success. Sam and I both knew we couldn't resolve the unhappiness in our lives without looking at it more closely. There was only one way to proceed: forward without hesitation.

"As far as I can see," I answered, "our discontent has clearly pointed us in one direction: to explore our potential." With that said, I still didn't have any ideas about how to proceed. I was about to lament this fact when Sam interrupted.

"Maybe the question is the answer," he pointed out, looking straight at me as though he had had a revelation.

"Sounds a little Zen," I replied. It was my turn to be sarcastic.

"Well, maybe it is," he answered, ignoring my tone of voice. "Our discontent has brought us to this point—your discontent with your work and my tiredness and overall malaise. We are sitting here together and we have explored it. And what have we decided? We have decided that the way forward is to allow our feelings of unhappiness to show us the way."

I nodded.

"What if the way forward is to some place we have never known before?" he continued. "Isn't that what we were saying, that we can use our dissatisfaction to figure out the answers when they are different from our usual way of thinking? If so, our potentials must lie somewhere beyond what we know, somewhere beyond the ways we conceive of

— ACCEPT your discontent
— EXAMINE your discontent
— take DECISIVE action as needed

EXPLORE THE POWER OF YOUR DISCONTENT

the world. Our possibilities lie buried in the unknown. And our very own dissatisfaction has brought us to the brink of this place."

I nodded some more.

When Sam talked about the unknown it conjured up images of a vast, dark, and cold landscape in my mind. I suspected that we would struggle in the unknown. But I also felt that it could be a rich and fertile land in which our potentials could become our tangible and enjoyable realities. It somehow reminded me of the time when we had just graduated from college. We both had big dreams and aspirations, but we really had no idea what was awaiting us in this unknown world beyond. In fact, looking back to that time, there was really no way for us to know. All we could do then was step into a new world. Perhaps it was time for us to do so again.

We didn't know what our discontent was pointing to, but it had become abundantly clear that the only way we would find out was by venturing into this unknown place.

POWER STEP ONE
Explore the Power of Your Discontent

FIVE POWER STEPS TIP

Once you accept and examine your discontent, you will come to a decision point. You will have faced the fact that you are not satisfied with some aspect of your situation, and you will have the choice to make a change. Many people falter at this stage, thinking they need to know what change they should be making and refusing to move ahead if they don't. In fact, the only decision required is a decision to want to make a change. What that change will look like remains to be discovered in the unknown.

NOTE : I relied on my job and achievements
Past : to give my life meaning. My marriage
to Lois was not satisfying. It lacked
the love and passion I wanted. My
religion no longer provided the meaning
and guidance I sought from it.

Changes needed to be made, and we were coming to terms with the fact that the nature of these changes lay hidden in unknown territory, waiting to be discovered. We had to leave our comfort zones and venture out.

Sam was the first to take the step. "What I want is to feel alive—you know?—really alive. I want to regain the energy I had before all of this started. I want to live a life filled with passion." He stirred his coffee. "I don't think it's going to be easy, but it's what I want."

I could see now that the picture-perfect life Sam had been leading was based on Sam being a certain Sam. It was based on Sam the businessman and rugged individualist. It was based on Sam focusing on being a success. It was also based on Sam living with a continuous feeling of fundamental discontent. To regain his energy, he needed to break out of this mold and find a new way to engage with the world.

The same held true for me. I was relying on my job to give my life meaning. In fact, there was not much else in my life.

"I want the same thing." It was my turn to take the plunge. "I don't know what that life looks like or what I would do. But I know I want a life filled with work that I enjoy, that is more me. And I want richer relationships. I'm tired of being alone. For once, I would like to have the chance to meet someone special and have a real relationship."

It felt risky to state my hopes, but admitting my discontent and committing to move ahead into the unknown was an important step.

"Well, I have a feeling we're in for quite a ride," stated Sam matter-of-factly.

"Yup, I guess we are."

We sat for a minute to digest what we had talked about that day. It was as though, by looking at our feelings of discontent, we had peered through the cracks in our lives. What we saw were promises of change and unknown outcomes ahead. We looked at each other for a moment, and we both knew that we had decided. There was nothing to do but move forward. We had asked ourselves: Is this all there is? And the answer was clear: No, there was more to life than this, and we wanted all of it.

What am I dissatisfied with in my life?

THE FIRST POWER STEP:
Explore the Power of Your Discontent

Exploring your discontent is not easy. It requires you to face the reality of your situation with honesty and directness. However, the results of the process are worthwhile.

To take a small step toward understanding your discontent, try the following exercise.

Make sure you have about thirty minutes to yourself in a comfortable and private setting. Take a piece of paper and divide it into two columns. Allow your thoughts to wander freely as you consider the following question: What are you discontent with in your life? Allow any thoughts to arise. Your thoughts could be about something big, like a relationship, your work, your financial situation, and so on. Or they could be about smaller things, like the décor in your home, the kind of car you drive, or what you have for lunch everyday.

Similar to a brainstorming activity, there are no wrong answers here. Write down your discontents in the left-hand column. After about fifteen minutes, or whenever you feel your list is complete, stop and review what you've written. How do you feel about it? In the right-hand column, next to each discontent you have listed, write down the emotions or experiences that describe that particular discontent. Perhaps you feel tired or frustrated or overwhelmed when you look at your discontents. Perhaps you feel indifferent or like they're not that important.

Review your output again. What does it say about the way you are experiencing your life right now?

THE FIRST POWER STEP AT A GLANCE

STEP 1: Explore the Power of Your Discontent

＊ Do not fear discontent. It is a signpost pointing you in the direction of your greatest possibilities.

＊ Use the power of your discontent to propel you ahead in an exploration of your potential.

＊ Seize the opportunity to stop and explore your discontent to discover your most important thoughts and feelings.

＊ Don't ignore discontent. If ignored, discontent can escalate to problems and crises. If explored, discontent becomes a powerful invitation to discover an opportunity for positive change.

＊ Accept discontent as an invitation to begin the Second Power Step: Face the Power of the Unknown.

TWO

THE SECOND POWER STEP:
Face the Power of the Unknown

When Sam and I left Lynn's Diner that day after our discussion about venturing into unfamiliar territory, I felt excited and hopeful. Perhaps there was something that could be done about getting out of my rut after all. But I had no further revelations during the week that followed. Experiencing my discontent had brought me to the doorstep of the unknown, but understanding how to get from where I was to where I wanted to go seemed outside my reach. I had to keep reminding myself that the very purpose of my discontent was to get me to engage with the opportunity to make some real changes in my life. In fact, I felt a little anxious about what lay ahead all week. But I could see that taking the time to discover and explore my thoughts with Sam had been helpful already, and I was committed to staying the course.

I was deeply in thought about this over a cup of coffee at Lynn's when Sam showed up. Our weekly lunch wasn't scheduled until the next day, but I had needed some time to contemplate what we had talked about, and so had headed down to the diner after a late afternoon appointment. It turned out Sam felt an urgency to make progress as well. He had called my office and, learning that I was out for the rest of the day, knew where I might be found. He barged into the diner, stuffed full of excitement.

"I thought I might find you here," he exclaimed with an air of his past self-assuredness, which was, somehow, comforting to witness. "I've got it. I've figured out what's wrong with my life and how to deal with it!"

I was amazed. Less than a week ago we had shared our discontents—Sam's about his lack of passion and energy and mine about my work—and we had identified that we needed to venture into the unknown to discover new possibilities. I had made no progress; in fact, I was getting frustrated again about not having figured out the way to move ahead. I was stuck while Sam had already figured out what lay hidden in the unknown. His lack of energy did not keep him from moving as fast as usual and I was jealous of it.

"I figured it out last night, Ron. I figured it out."

My old envy for Sam's charge-ahead attitude and magnetism for success had returned. How did he do it? How was he able to make decisions and push forward so simply? The more I thought about the conundrum of my career, the more I felt imprisoned in my thoughts. However, my hesitation did not seem to dampen Sam's enthusiasm for his epiphany.

"I am going to sell the business," he explained. "I will sell the whole thing off. I will have nothing to do with it anymore. I am going to set myself free and take the time to repair my relationship with Mary-Jane. I value her and my freedom so much more than anything else I have!" He beamed at me, elated with his decision.

For a moment, I thought that he had, indeed, figured out how to move forward. What a revelation! What a radical change! But as he elaborated on his plan, I felt a growing sense of unease. In fact, I soon realized I was not remotely convinced by the result of his exploration.

First, as far as I knew, Mary-Jane had not married a guy who would hang around the house to dwell on the ways and whiles of their relationship. In fact, she was hardly home herself! As an active professional woman in her own right, Mary-Jane had a career and friendships and a social life that required her attention. She had married a man who was, like her, an outgoing, fun, and spirited entrepreneur with a sense of accomplishment and direction. The last thing she probably needed was a constant companion who suddenly had no goals other than to spend time with her.

Second, apart from giving him more time to spend with Mary-Jane, selling his business didn't seem to have any other benefits. I knew Sam loved that business. He had spent years growing it from a small shop to a major business with rapidly growing potential. I had understood that, as with any growing business, the possibility of selling the chain had always been an option, but only when the time was right and the move made sense. To waste the true potential of his business with one swift change of his mind simply didn't sit well with me.

Sam looked at me expectantly. After his outburst and accompanying explanation, he was looking for acceptance from his companion in crime. "That's great, Sam," I said, but I suspect we both knew I was lying. I couldn't think of anything else to say. An uncomfortable silence grew around the table.

"What?" Sam asked, sounding irritated. "You don't like what I've come up with?"

I still didn't know what to say. He had obviously been excited by the idea. Who was I to suggest it wasn't the right course of action? Yet, I reminded myself, we had made a commitment to be honest as we explored our potential. Withholding my true thoughts would not help the situation. Finally, I took the leap.

"To be honest, Sam," I replied, "you're right. I don't like it. I don't think you've hit on the answer to unraveling your discontent with this idea."

He swallowed. I don't think he had expected me to be quite so frank in my assessment. I continued nonetheless. I cared about Sam too much to let him go down that road.

"It's just that it seems like such an impulsive decision. It seems like you're hoping to get rid of your unhappiness by doing away with one source of stress."

Sam looked disgruntled. "Of course I want to get rid of my discontent," he replied passionately. "I mean, that's the whole point of this exercise, isn't it, to get beyond this tiredness and frustration? If I need to make a big change, I'm not afraid. I'm willing to take the plunge."

Once again, Sam was convincing in his arguments. When he felt strongly about something, it was easy to buckle under the pressure of his convictions. I struggled to find a way to explain my unease. We had entered the unknown together and neither of us was an authority on this subject, this much was clear.

"I don't know, Sam. I guess if it takes a big change, then it takes a big change. I like that you've broken out of the mold to consider other options. But is it possible that you're trying to take the easy way out? To get rid of your discontent, are you really willing to get rid of everything else you've built at the same time?"

Sam was silent.

I thought for a minute, stirred my coffee, and continued. "I admire you for daring to step into the unknown so boldly. All I've done is sit around and ponder, with no results whatsoever." We both had to smile at my confession. "I just think it would be worthwhile for you to look at things a little more closely."

Sam sighed. I suspected he knew in his heart of hearts that I was right.

"Well," Sam sighed again, "You're probably right. I suppose if I really ended up selling the business now, my unhappiness wouldn't just go away. I mean there is a big part of me that still likes to run this business and I have worked so hard to get it to where it is." He paused. "So what do I do? Just sit around and wait?"

He was visibly frustrated and I could easily understand why. Sam was a go-getter. Waiting went against his nature.

"We're not talking about waiting," I replied. "We're talking about being willing to understand what our discontent is really signaling. To take action without understanding the real possibilities ahead may cause us to miss out on those possibilities. I think that an exploration of the unknown takes more effort than we've given it so far."

Sam sighed again. "If you say so," he grumbled, but there was a smirk on his face as he did. "You suddenly seem to know how to make your way through this." It was a friendly jab, but it worked. I blushed. It was obvious that I was winging my way through this process as much as he was.

"You got me Sam," I said. It was my turn to sigh. "The truth is that I feel stuck with this as much as you do. And I find it just as frustrating."

Just then, Lynn appeared at our table to check on us.

"Still pondering the meaning of life?" She smiled at us as she topped up my mug with steaming hot coffee and poured a fresh cup for Sam.

"Yup," I replied. "We may need more coffee."

We all laughed.

"No problem," said Lynn. "Come by anytime. If you're going to figure out the meaning of life, this is the place to do it."

POWER STEP TWO
Face the Power of the Unknown

Too many people make radical decisions simply to escape their feelings of unhappiness. However, you do not always have to make a radical change in your life to deal with an experience of discontent. Rather, you can take the time to allow the discontent to lead you to discover something fundamentally new about yourself and your situation. Once you have made this discovery, you can take effective action. Until then, your actions may actually serve to compound your problems.

We laughed again. Sam and I talked for a while longer, but we moved no closer toward solving anything. We decided to keep our regular lunch date at the diner the next day. At the rate we were going, we decided we could use the time and the support we were finding in each other.

✳ ✳ ✳

The next day, Sam came prepared with ideas. Good ideas.

"Ron, my man," he greeted me jovially. "Listen, I've been thinking, and here is what I want to talk about."

"You don't waste any time, Sam." We both laughed at how passionate we had become.

"Seriously, Ron. Last night I thought more about why you didn't like my idea of selling my business. I think you were trying to tell me that I should allow the process of facing the unknown to take its course, and that selling the business really wasn't a step out of the familiar. It was more like shuffling my cards around rather than dealing myself a whole new hand."

He had put my feelings into words perfectly. "Exactly, that's what I was trying to say."

Sam continued. "Well, I think you had a good point. Selling my business would be a radical step. So last night I thought about it some more and I asked myself why I had come up with this idea. And I realized something: selling my business would change my circumstances, but it would also change who I am. I mean, I am a businessman, first and foremost. If I sold the business for the purpose of spending more time on my relationship, I would have to look at myself differently."

I was impressed. "Sam, that makes so much sense." I was suddenly excited; Sam seemed to have figured out a critical part of exploring the unknown and I sensed a breakthrough in our struggles. "It's like selling the business is a way of changing who you are. So maybe the most important part of your idea is about changing who you are, not selling the business. Perhaps your perception of who you are needs to change before you can really discover what lies ahead."

Sam nodded. "Yeah, that's the sense I got last night. How I see myself—you know, as a businessman for example—gives me a predictable way to manage my life. It's my identity. Maybe our identities have to change or get bigger before we can discover our potentials."

Maybe our discontent is telling us that our identities need to be upgraded.

I jumped in. "Say in your case, Sam, your identity consists of being a husband, being a businessman, being of a certain cultural background, being wealthy, being a golfer, and so on. By creating an identity, it's as though you have created a zone of comfort that you're familiar with. Your identity helps you to solve problems and relate to other people. It's like a handle with which to manage your life situation. It allows you to have a predictable and consistent way of being. But, at the same time, it confines you."

"I think that's right," agreed Sam, "but I think the problem arises when we value our identities more than the changes we need to make in our lives. Changes are threatening. It's almost like we start to defend our identities rather than allow them to evolve."

I thought about Sam's point and it seemed to make sense. "Yes," I responded, "and when you say, 'This is who I am,' you are asserting your status quo identity rather than facing a required change. I'm starting to think that our current identities are not serving our needs completely."

"Maybe our discontent is telling us that our identities—how we see ourselves and the world, our fundamental handles to deal with our lives—need to be upgraded."

I was excited. "If this is true, we're struggling in the unknown because it feels difficult, if not impossible, to break out of our comfort zones. How can my life really change? How can I break out of the rut I'm in at work? How can your relationship with Mary-Jane improve? We may not be able to answer any of these questions as long as we remain in our comfort zones. In fact, remaining in our comfort zones might prevent the solutions from entering our awareness. Our identities are, in a sense, imprisoning us in states of discontent."

We were on fire now. I continued. "We can't find the

answers to our questions at this point, because any answers that arise right now are coming from our current identities, right?"

Sam paused before adding to my point.

"I think that's right. From the current vantage points of our identities, we can see only what we have always seen. How can we possibly discover new opportunities if we are looking with the same eyes from the same points of view?

POWER STEP TWO
Face the Power of the Unknown

To discover something fundamentally new about yourself, you first have to face the unknown. The unknown is the place where your identity can change. Think of yourself as a particular person with a particular set of abilities and challenges. This is the identity that allows you to deal with your life in a predictable manner. This identity also becomes a prison if you do not realize that it needs to change and expand. You can use your time in the unknown to evaluate, understand, and evolve your concept of who you think you are.

You're right. We need to allow our identities to shift before we'll be able to find different approaches to the questions we're wrestling with."

At this moment we understood the importance of exploring the uncharted territory of the unknown for the first time. We couldn't find a fundamentally relevant solution to our problems because all the answers were arising from a way of being and a way of thinking that had been crystalized into our identities. The discontent we were experiencing had arisen as a result of situations that forced us to bump up against the glass walls of our identities. The only way to move forward effectively was to realize how our views of the world and of ourselves needed to change. But the way forward remained hidden in the unknown. We would find the answers to our questions only once we stepped fully into the unknown.

"I'm glad you were so convinced about having to sell your business," I teased Sam. "Without that, we may never have figured this out!"

Sam laughed. "It's like we need to talk about and explore who we think we are before we can discover who we want to be. I guess that means we'll just be hanging around in the unknown for now," he quipped.

"Yup," I agreed. "Let's see what exploring the unknown will bring for us."

Time had passed quickly and work was calling. We paid our bill and left the diner together with the unspoken agreement that we would both stick with the plan to learn about our current identities and how they might be constraining our exploration of our possibilities. I was certain that we would now make good progress.

✳ ✳ ✳

Sam later confessed to me that this stage of the whole process was the most difficult for him. He came up with idea after idea for solving his predicament: Sell the business. Grow the business. Partner with someone else to manage the business. Take courses in something artsy, say photography. No, better yet, take a few months off for a golf vacation. Or to go fishing. Or, no, to travel. Take Mary-Jane on a cruise. Maybe see a professional? In his own words, once he fully entered the unknown, Sam was a mess. Not only had he admitted his discontent, he was now lost in a sea of thoughts about what he could or should do to deal with it.

It was in the middle of this exploration that Sam received a phone call from his sister, Sarah, who lived in New York. She worked for an international aid organization supporting children's education; she was raising funds for a new project and was calling to ask for Sam's help. He told me later that he was surprised at his reaction to the call. He was shorter with her than was called for, and, while he made a donation, his preoccupation with the questions of his own discontent seemed so much more important. He had to figure out what to do next with his life, and he simply did not have time for Sarah's project. Much later, we laughed about this particular moment in time. After all, he had had a chance right then to discover his potential, but he had passed up the opportunity because he was too busy exploring his options!

As for me, I was about ready to toss it all in. None of the ideas I came up with to address my discontent seemed worthy of pursuing. Like Sam, I had a constant list of possibilities circulating in my head. Should I leave my job? Start my own consulting company? Find a different employer? Maybe even go back to school? And how would I ever find a partner? Should I join a singles club? Or get whatever friends I had left to find me a blind date? Much like Sam, I felt incapacitated with my thoughts, and any action seemed impossible. The theory about identity that Sam and I had discussed during our last meeting did not seem to help me; I was stuck in a rut more than ever.

Sam and I had agreed that our current identities were comfortable places that we needed to leave to find the answers to our discontent. But what exactly was so comfortable about this place was beginning to elude me completely. My frustration grew. Wading about in the unknown was not the adventure I had thought it might be. As far as I was concerned, the next meeting with Sam couldn't come soon enough.

When at last the meeting date did arrive, Sam and I talked well into the afternoon. The pile of paperwork on my desk had to wait; Sam did not make any movement toward his office that afternoon, either.

We were passionately discussing our different views on the topic when Sam asked an important question: "So what is the unknown?" Sam's question rang challengingly in the diner's afternoon silence for a few moments before dissolving into the room.

"I have no idea," I said, and finally we had cause to laugh. It was a relief to admit that I didn't know the answer.

"Seriously, though," I continued, "we've agreed that new ideas and solutions do not arise from what we already know. As long as we insist on having the answers to our questions, we are operating in the realm of our current identities. However evolved and advanced these identities may be, however hard we have worked to get to where we are, our current identities are merely fractions of our possibilities as individuals."

Sam nodded.

"The unknown, then, is nothing but a process that helps us expand our identities and our senses of self. It is really a process that guides us to the discovery of other aspects of our potentials. No, more than that. It is a fundamental and necessary part of the process to discover who we are and what we are capable of."

Sam pulled out a notebook and opened it to a page filled with writing. It looked as though he had been doing his homework since our last meeting—more than could be said for me.

"What's this now, Sam?" I asked, waving to Lynn for another cup of coffee.

"Well, last week got me thinking about this idea of making a change. I started writing down all sorts of ideas for where my life might go. I hoped it might help me figure things out."

Sam showed me a table of neatly arranged columns and rows. I hadn't done anything of the sort. Perhaps I was more the brooding kind. I had certainly thought about similar questions over the past week, but outlining these questions in a neat, tabulated fashion as Sam had done seemed much more effective.

"Basically, I listed all my options and priorities here"— Sam pointed to the left portion of his table—"and then list-

> **POWER STEP TWO**
> **Face the Power of the Unknown**
>
> **FIVE POWER STEPS TIP**
>
> It is important to remind yourself that many of the challenges in your situation arise from the status quo of your established identity. As long as you insist on having the answers to your questions already, you are effectively closing the door to the unknown. By allowing yourself the freedom to wait until a relevant answer arises, you have the opportunity to make a meaningful and significant discovery about yourself and your situation. Do not insist on having the answers already. If you do, the door to your greatest possibilities may remain locked.

ed all the pros and cons over here." He pointed to the right and nodded with seeming assuredness that he had, indeed, covered everything.

"Take a look," Sam said, passing the paper to me, "and tell me what you think."

I looked at the table that Sam had prepared, expecting to have been left behind in tackling this project yet again, as had seemed to be the case a number of times over the past few weeks. But when I started to read, I realized it was only a listing of his usual options. Sell the business, keep the business, spend more time with Mary-Jane, take up a new hobby or sport. We had gone over these before. There was nothing on the list that would force Sam out of his comfort zone and into a position where he could discover something significant or new about the next step in his life.

To my relief, Sam commented on the shortcomings of the list himself. "Do you see what this is?" Sam's frustrations were evident. "It's the same old list of the same old solutions. This theory about discontent and the unknown is all nice and good. But how does it apply? I mean how will it get me to where I need to go? Obviously, no matter what I do or think about, I come up with the same old solutions."

As I reviewed Sam's list, I had an idea. What if we couldn't think our way into the future? What if we had to use our imaginations and our senses to discover a new way forward? I remembered an exercise I had used in management meetings. Would it help Sam and me find our way out of the quagmire we'd found ourselves in?

"I have an idea, Sam." I decided we should at least give it a try.

"Great," he mumbled, "I'm up for anything that will get me out of this place of waiting and seeing and onto the next step."

We both had to laugh at his grumbling.

I started to explain what I was talking about. "Okay, so we're clear we have stepped into the unknown. We're clear we don't know the answer. Not even if we write all of our options down on paper."

I nodded at his page with a smile, and Sam shrugged his shoulders with another disgruntled sigh.

"Maybe what we need to do is imagine our way through the unknown," I continued. "We can't think our way through the unknown, because we would be proceeding from the same identities as before. What if we imagined what might be possible and began to explore the unknown around us a little more?"

I drew a dot in the middle of an empty page in Sam's notebook. Then I drew a small circle around the dot, and a larger circle around that one. As I did, I began to explain.

"Let's assume that the dot is where you are now. And let's assume the small circle is where you will be in two years, and the bigger circle is where you will be in five years."

Sam nodded. He seemed to be interested in the new approach.

"So we guess where we will be?" he asked. "Or we decide where we will be? Or we set goals for where we will be?"

"Well," I replied, "when I get clients to do this exercise, I first get them to brainstorm possibilities for where their

> ## POWER STEP TWO
> ### Face the Power of the Unknown
>
>
> FIVE POWER STEPS TIP
>
> To begin exploring the unknown you can employ your imagination. Your imagination has the capacity to transcend your limited identity and it can operate in the unknown. You can use your senses to feel the experiences that would result if you evolved your identity. What would it look and feel like to be different? Imagine in your mind a scenario of what is possible. Imagine what this scenario might feel like. Employ your imagination to open the door to your greatest possibilities.

businesses would be in two years or five years or whenever. I think this approach would work in our situation as well, but I was thinking we would actually do it twice."

"Twice?"

"Yes, twice. We talked about how our identities are our comfort zones, but really they are uncomfortable once we have outgrown them. So let's do this twice. The first time around, let's imagine we continue with our current identities. The second time, let's imagine we are able to evolve our identities and operate from new and improved platforms. Let's try to imagine where we'll end up."

"Okay, makes sense," Sam nodded.

"You go first," I declared.

"All right, so I suppose we're asking what my life might be like in two years if things remain the same?" This wasn't an easy question to answer, and Sam gave it some serious thought.

"Make sure you imagine continuing with your same identity in the same way you have been," I reminded him. "Where do you end up?"

He took a breath and continued to think. Finally, he spoke. "I think the truth is that my marriage may not last another couple of years if things continue as they are." This was a tough thing to say, as I could tell by his face and the flash of sadness that came over it.

"Mary-Jane and I might be headed for divorce. The business would probably be doing all right—though I imagine I might not have much passion for it anymore—but I don't think Mary-Jane and I would make it. I think it would be a tough time." Sam looked at me and sighed. "This certainly brings the point home, doesn't it?"

I nodded. The disappointment on Sam's face was visible. I couldn't think of anything to say. There was a brief silence before Sam continued.

"The more I think about this scenario, the more certain I become that it is not what I want. To let my relationship fall apart and be left with nothing but a business I'm not passionate about is not what I want. There must be more to my life than this. Something has to change. Something will change. I will not let things go on as they are now."

I was heartened to see Sam make a decision to move ahead, even if he didn't know how. The feeling around the table was heavy, and I thought it best to shift gears.

"Do you want to have another run at this?" I suggested. "This time, let's assume that you find a way through the unknown, that you continue to explore your discontent, and that you take the steps necessary to discover a finer, stronger, better version of Sam." *There must be a finer, stronger, better version of me.*

Sam laughed, but I persisted. "Let's basically assume you stick with the process we've been discussing for the past few weeks. What do you imagine your life will be like in two years?" *How do I do that?*

Again, Sam thought for a while before speaking.

"Well, I would like to see my relationship work out." This was still a difficult subject to broach, but Sam seemed determined to imagine a different outcome. He thought about the question some more. "Yes, that is definitely one of the things that I want. But I feel as though something else is missing here. I mean, I want my relationship to work out, but I also want my life, in general, to be about something more. Things have gone stagnant for me. It's like I need to discover something that will not only rejuvenate my relationship, but also my life." He sighed again. "Trouble is, I have no idea what it is."

I would like to see me heal mentally, emotionally, physically and spiritually. I would like to see me prosper in all areas of my life.

43

I looked at him. I wasn't about to let him give up this easily. "Well, maybe you don't need to know what it is right now. Maybe that's still ahead for you to discover. Let's just assume that you've figured out how to move ahead. What might your life feel like in a couple of years?"

Sam stirred his coffee quietly. "If I could make it through the un-known and discover the missing pieces?"

I nodded.

He considered the question for a few more minutes. I could tell from the look on his face that he was slowly realiz-ing something. He gave me a quizzical look.

POWER STEP TWO
Face the Power of the Unknown

Once you come to understand your identity and its limitations, it is easier to open the door to your greatest possibilities. It becomes clear that the current status of who you are is simply no longer suitable, and that explor-ing how you can experience the world differently is the only way forward. This realization consti-tutes your commitment to exploring what is really possible. By understanding the limitations of your identity, you open the door and step through to discov-ering the power of your potential.

"Well, if I could really figure it out, I believe I would feel sort of calm, I think, and peaceful. Passionate. Happy. Whatever I might be doing would be surrounded by these feelings. It's quite a nice sensation, actually. It's like the search has ended and I've discovered something fundamen-tal. It's like I have discovered the real source of satisfaction and meaning in my life." He looked up at me. "These feel-ings could rejuvenate my relationship and life in general."

I took a deep breath. We had finally hit onto something.

"Do you actually feel this way right now, I mean, right in this moment?" I asked, curious.

Sam nodded, a surprised and happy look on his face. "I do."

"Sam," I said, "this is good. Although we don't know what will happen or what we will discover, it seems like you now have a sense of what you would like your new experience—your new identity—to feel like. Maybe this is another signpost that can guide you through your next steps."

Sam nodded to himself.

"Yes, it seems like I could create some interesting new experiences if I felt like this more often. I mean, as I'm feeling this way I can imagine myself having a good relationship with Mary-Jane, and actually having a lot of fun together. And I can imagine myself doing something interesting besides what I'm doing now with the business."

He nodded again.

"Yeah, I still can't really imagine what that might be, but I just know there is something waiting for me. There is something new I can discover about my life and just knowing that feels good."

He paused, and then looked at me with a smile. "So what do you want your life to be like in a few years?"

I shrugged my shoulders as Lynn placed a cup of coffee in front of me. Picking up the steaming mug, I responded with a sigh: "I wish I knew."

THE SECOND POWER STEP:
Face the Power of the Unknown

Facing the unknown can be a challenge because it requires you to consider that you may not have the answers just yet. An effective way to facilitate a successful encounter with the unknown is to use your imagination in a similar way to how Ron instructed Sam in this chapter.

Take about thirty minutes to yourself in a private and comfortable setting with little interruption. You will need some paper and a pen. Make a dot in the middle of your page and draw a circle around it. Divide this pie into pieces that correspond to some of the key areas in your life. For example, you may want to label one piece of the pie "money," another "relationship," a third "health," and so on. For a few minutes, imagine what each of these pieces of the pie would contain if you continued with your life unchanged for the next two years. How do you feel about your life ahead if you do not make a change? For another few minutes, consider what might be possible in each of these pieces of the pie if you stepped into the unknown, discovered something new and important about yourself, your interests, and your abilities, and actively pursued this discovery for two years. Note down the most important ideas, images, and feelings in the relevant piece of the pie. Review what you have on the page. How do you feel about the potential of your life situation?

THE SECOND POWER STEP AT A GLANCE

STEP 2: Face the Power of the Unknown

＊ Do not rush through the unknown. It is necessary to experience the unknown fully to discover new possibilities.

＊ Use your time in the unknown to evaluate, understand, and evolve your identity.

＊ Do not insist on having the answers already. If you do, the door to the unknown will remain locked.

＊ Employ your imagination to open the door to the unknown. Use your senses to feel the experiences that would result if you evolved your identity.

＊ Open the door to the unknown and step through to the Third Power Step: Discover the Power of Your Potential.

THREE

THE THIRD POWER STEP:
Discover the Power of Your Potential

During the week that followed the visioning exercise I'd led Sam through, I pondered what my life would be like if I could find a way to maneuver through the unknown. As I had the week before, I waited for our next meeting to arrive with great anticipation.

Sam was waiting for me in our usual booth when I opened the door to Lynn's Diner. As I made my way to join him, I waved at Lynn for my usual order, and she acknowledged me with a smile.

"How are you doing?" Sam looked at me with a questioning look as I shuffled into the booth.

"Remember the exercise we did last week?" I asked. "Remember the feeling you had when you considered moving forward in a new direction?"

Sam nodded. "It was kind of a peaceful feeling; clear and quiet. I couldn't get it out of my mind all week—it felt so different from my usual busy life."

"I completed the same exercise after our last meeting, and I had the same feeling. I thought we had finally opened the door to something important. The trouble is, the feeling didn't last long. I mean, I still don't really know which way to go from here."

My frustration was obvious. I had glimpsed what my life might be like, yet, in reality, nothing had changed. My discontent was still there.

"I know what you mean," replied Sam. "The same thing happened to me."

The frustration must have showed on our faces when Lynn wandered over with our coffees in hand. "Are you guys at it again?" she laughed with a happy smile.

"Yup," I said with a feeble attempt at humor, "still figuring out the meaning of life." I don't know if it was the tired tone in my voice or something else that prompted her to slide into our booth, or if she had been planning it all along. Regardless, Lynn placed the coffee pot on the table and sat down next to Sam without any invitation.

"Listen boys," she said, "I don't mean to barge in, but I just can't stand your long faces anymore. I've been hearing you guys talk about making some changes for weeks, but it doesn't look like you're doing so well."

"We're making some headway…" Sam started.

"Speak for yourself," I added, and we finally laughed that day.

"It looks to me like you boys could use some help figuring this thing out," Lynn said matter-of-factly. She looked at us with her persistent smile.

"And you think you're the one to help us?" I asked. I was doubtful and, to be quite honest, slightly annoyed that Lynn had interrupted us so bluntly. I was about to ask Lynn to leave the booth so we could continue our conversation, when Sam interjected.

"Maybe she could help, Ron."

"Well," responded Lynn calmly, "it wouldn't hurt if I gave it a try, right?" She looked straight at me.

I shrugged my shoulders.

"I'm Lynn by the way." She held out her hand.

I reached over to shake her hand. "I'm Ron, and this is Sam."

Sam smiled at her and shook her hand as well.

"From what I've heard, you guys seem to be talking about where to go with your lives. How are you going about it?"

Sam answered for both of us. "We started with the fact that we both feel discontent; it was relatively easy to get that part out in the open.

POWER STEP THREE
Discover the Power of Your Potential

Because you are exploring new territory, it is important to receive feedback about your ideas and to learn how other people see your situation. When trying to break out of the confines of your identity, you will need all the help you can get. Do not hesitate to involve a community of people in discovering your potential.

Then we started talking about stepping outside of our comfort zones, you know, facing the unknown. We think that, to make a real change, we need to explore opportunities beyond the identities we normally operate from. We think we have figured out something important, but we've made very little progress in changing our lives so far, and it's getting frustrating."

"Well, isn't that the way it goes with most important things you do? I mean, sometimes the prep work can seem to take forever, but when you finally piece it all together, things can happen just like that." Lynn smiled at Sam. "Your idea about looking at your identities and stepping out of your comfort zones sounds interesting. Isn't it all about figuring out who you really are? That's what I've found in my life, at least."

"And why would what you have found in your life have anything to do with what we're going through?" I asked abruptly. The moment after I said these words, I regretted them. They were, quite simply, mean and unhelpful. But Lynn didn't seem to mind.

"I had to make some tough decisions and some fundamental changes in my life a few years back," she calmly said, "and when I did, I learned a few things about understanding myself and figuring out what I wanted."

I wondered what Lynn had been through. Whatever it had been, it seemed as though it had led her to make a major adjustment in her life.

Sam perked up. "Sounds exactly like what we're talking about as well. I think Lynn's right; maybe she can help us."

I felt significantly less excited than Sam. If Lynn had really discovered something so fundamental about her life, why was she still waiting tables at a diner? Then again, I reminded myself, I did not know what kind of challenges she had faced.

"Okay, okay," I conceded, "why don't you join us for a cup of coffee?"

"Why thank you for the kind invitation," she said. She waved at another waitress for another coffee cup, which was delivered promptly. Our meeting had taken an unexpected turn.

"So tell me more about this 'unknown' you mentioned. What's that all about?"

"Well," I answered, "we think that stepping out of our normal identities is like stepping into the unknown, and that we can't find our way through the unknown based on our usual thought processes. We believe we need to use our emotional and intuitive capacities as well."

Sam and I looked at each other with a shared sense of pride. Summarized like this, it seemed as if we had covered quite a bit of ground together after all.

"Sounds like you boys are well on your way then," Lynn commented. "So what's holding you up?"

Sam put it perfectly. "We know that aspects of our potentials are in the unknown somewhere. We know that we're missing parts of who we really are. We just don't know how to discover what those parts are!"

Lynn nodded. "That's a tough one." She paused for a couple of seconds before continuing, looking at her coffee cup. "I see a lot of people coming in and out of this diner. And what always strikes me is how many people are concerned with figuring out who they really are. So many people have the same question written across their faces."

She looked up. Her eyes were clear and bright.

"Everyone is looking for answers to their problems. And I always think that the biggest problem is that people focus on themselves too much. What do *I* want, where do *I* want to go, what do *I* want to do, what do *I* want to get. It's all about me, me, me. But I don't think that's the only place to look for answers."

Lynn's voice was soft, yet strong. I was becoming intrigued by what she was saying.

"If you ask me, when you're so busy looking at what you want and where you want to go, you're missing something important. You're missing the rest of who you are, because you're forgetting about the world you're in.

Without the world, there is no Ron or Sam or Lynn. If you don't consider the world, all of these thoughts about what you want and where you want to go are pointless. To discover your potential, you have to look up from your individual problems and out at the world."

This was beginning to make some sense to me and I was glad Lynn had joined us at the table.

There was a moment of silence around the table as Sam and I contemplated the importance of what Lynn had just said.

POWER STEP THREE

Discover the Power of Your Potential

It is necessary to look at your own feelings and thoughts quite closely to realize that you need to make a change in your situation. But to discover a new aspect of your potential, you need to look beyond yourself. Your greatest possibilities arise in relation to the world around you. Both you and the world around you are important components in discovering what matters in your situation. Look at yourself to get to the doorstep of your potential. Look at the world to discover your greatest possibilities.

Lynn took another sip of her coffee before continuing. "You know, a few years ago, I got some bad news. My doctors informed me that I was battling cancer. Within a few days I saw the rest of my life disappear before my eyes. I had to face the fact that my life might not be as I thought it would be. I had to face the fact that my own small existence was a lot more fragile than I had thought"

Lynn took another breath.

"I still remember telling my grandmother the news about my health at the time. She and I have always been really close and I'll never forget what she said. She just looked at me and said that, for most people, life is like being a single grain of sand on a vast beach. On the beach, there are billions of grains of sand, just like there are billions of people in our world. What can a single grain of sand do to make a difference? How can a single grain of sand find a meaningful existence? She said that most people live their lives as if they are just one of these grains of sand, with no influence over the bigger picture. And she said that living your life like that does not lead to happiness."

There was silence around the table. Lynn continued.

"I think my grandma was right. To discover your true potential you need to consider what solution could benefit you and the world at the same time. You need to look up and out and consider the world and its needs as much as you consider your own needs. As long as you focus only on what you want, you have cut yourself off from your greatest possibilities. But only focusing on the world doesn't work either. To discover who you truly are, you need to have the best interests of yourself *and* the world in mind."

She paused again.

"Grandma believed that we shouldn't go through our lives thinking we are just small grains of sand in a vast world. She thought we should live our lives as though we could make significant contributions to our world.

"To make a long story short," Lynn continued, "I was lucky. The cancer was caught at an early stage and, with some months of treatment, it receded. I've been fine for a good long while now, but my grandma's advice has stuck with me. The scare of facing how fragile my life was, and is, has left me with a new outlook on life. For a while, I thought my life was ending and that it had been meaning-less. Now, I always try to see the bigger picture of what is going on. And when I look around me, I am struck by how many people see themselves as that single grain of sand that has little impact on things."

There was another quiet moment around the table. Finally, Sam cleared his throat and spoke.

"I'm glad to hear you're better," he commented. "I mean, I can see how such a scare can change the way you see things."

I nodded quietly. Sam continued.

"But really, I mean, when it comes to this idea of having an impact on your world, isn't it the reality of an individ-ual's life to be the grain of sand—one person surrounded by billions of other people?"

I nodded at Lynn. The idea that we may be too focused on ourselves, and that we were limited by this focus, intrigued me. Lynn had opened the door to a bigger concept than we had thought about before.

"Yeah, I know what Sam means," I said. "Just to make sure I understand, are you saying that we have been looking at ourselves as having limited possibilities? You're saying we have to look at ourselves as part of a larger community?"

"Well, I think it's even more than that. Yes, you're a part of a larger community. But within that community, it's like you have a lot more power and potential than you think. We need to discover who we are in relation to the world around us. Our reach can actually extend far beyond what we think is possible. I think you guys are right about needing to step into the unknown to discover what is possible. If you care to, you actually have the chance to discover possibilities far beyond what you can now imagine."

I was stunned. For weeks we had sat here in this small

diner, and Lynn had indirectly been part of our meetings each time. I had never expected her to be remotely interested in the kinds of questions we'd been discussing, let alone throw open the door to the most important question we had to answer to resolve our discontent.

There was silence at our table after Lynn finished her explanation. Lynn got up to fill some-

POWER STEP THREE

Discover the Power of Your Potential

FIVE POWER STEPS TIP

Discovering your potential requires you to ask some fundamental questions about who you are and the values and ideas you care about. It is of great importance to be as open as possible to new ideas about who you might become, and what you might find important and meaningful in your life. To discover your greatest possibilities, ask yourself, "Who am I?" and take into account the big picture when you answer.

one's coffee cup, but Sam and I remained quiet, each deep in our own thoughts.

Finally, I broke the silence. "So the question is simple: who are you?"

"I agree," said Sam. "The question is simple. But it sounds like the answer is bigger than we thought it would be. Our new identities could provide a whole new and different answer to this question. Who am I? What do I care about? What really matters to me? Who am I beyond the roles and responsibilities of my current situation? What could I accomplish if I reached out beyond being just one of a billion grains of sand on this beach called life? Once you decide to expand your identity, almost anything is possible."

I nodded. There was a lot to think about now. The door to our potentials had been thrown wide open. Suddenly, new possibilities could arise. Suddenly, we could see the way forward. There was nothing else to say.

"Let's go," I said. Sam nodded. Somewhat dazed, we got up and left our money on the table. Lynn waved at us on our way out, and we waved back.

"Who is she, anyway?" said Sam at the door step.

I looked back at Lynn as I responded. "Whoever she is, I think she just saved us in there."

* * *

In the days that followed, I thought a lot about what Lynn had said. The whole world could open up to me if I was willing to reconsider my narrow self-concept. Not only might I discover a solution to my discontent, but a fundamental aspect of my potential as a person.

For weeks, I had felt guilty that I wasn't able to be more helpful to Sam. After all, he had originally called me for my supposed expertise in helping with change. In reality, I felt like I'd been struggling more than him. After our last meeting at Lynn's, however, it began to occur to me that my expertise had very little to do with our situation.

In excited anticipation for our next meeting, I shifted my schedule for the week to make sure that I would have enough time for another extended lunch at Lynn's. But the day before our next get-together, Sam left me a message. It was short and sounded hurried. He said he was otherwise occupied and would have to miss this week's meeting at the diner.

I tried calling him a couple of times during the following week, but to no avail. The days felt endless and I still felt stuck, although amidst my hesitation and the complications of moving forward, I began to feel an underlying sense of confidence and excitement. I sensed that the opportunity to leap ahead was close at hand.

When a second meeting date passed and I still hadn't heard from Sam, I began to get concerned. Both he and Mary-Jane could not be reached at home, and all I reached at Sam's office was his voice mail. I had begun to worry seriously about Sam's whereabouts when my cell phone rang.

"Are we on for this week?" It was Sam. A different-sounding Sam, but Sam.

"Where have you been?" I demanded. "And why do you sound so happy? I was getting worried about you!"

"Just got back from Hawaii," said Sam, "with Mary-Jane. I've got some news for you."

A vacation! For a brief second, jealousy and anger started to get the better of me—I could have used a vacation too! But my surprise surpassed my jealousy. First, I knew that Sam never took time off. But even more surprising was the fact that he had taken time off with Mary-Jane. Sam had confided that their relationship had been getting even staler throughout the time we'd been meeting. A spontaneous two-week vacation in romantic Hawaii was an unexpected development.

"I'll see you at Lynn's tomorrow," said Sam, and he hung up.

"See you there," I mumbled into the dial tone, unsure of what was to come.

I slept restlessly that night, and I arrived early for our lunch meeting the next day. I had just sat down in our usual booth, anxious to discover what had taken Sam out of town so unexpectedly, when Lynn came by the table, smiling.

"I missed you boys," she said as she placed a coffee before me. "It's good to have you back. It's not often I get to have a reasonable conversation in this diner. How are you doing?"

"I'm still not making much progress," I replied. At least I could be honest about it. "But Sam says he has something to share."

"Well, keep me posted," she replied as she moved to the next table. I sat for a few more minutes, waiting impatiently for Sam. I looked over each time the door opened, until, at last, he arrived. And just behind him was Mary-Jane.

POWER STEP THREE
Discover the Power of Your Potential

Everyone has a different way of discovering their potential. Some people discover it early. Some take longer. Some people discover it through experience, others through introspection. For some, it means a radical life shift, for others a quiet confirmation of their path as it is and an acceptance of their circumstances. Your potential is as unique as you are. Don't simply copy what other people are doing to reach their potential. You can discover a way that works for you.

I had grown a lot closer to Sam since he and I had started to meet at Lynn's Diner, but I hadn't had a chance to see Mary-Jane. In fact, I hadn't seen her since a brief encounter we'd had at a local mall a few years earlier.

She looked fantastic, with two weeks of Hawaii behind her and a happy man beside her. Sam looked radiant, like a new man.

Perhaps what struck me most was how good they looked together. They had an air of softness and happiness about them, like people who had rediscovered each other. Their ten-year marriage had the look of new love. Seeing them come into the diner looking this way ended my bout of jealousy. There was nothing to be jealous about. Sam had faced his situation and had come to an important realization. I couldn't wait to hear what it was.

Soon after we'd exchanged hellos and settled into our regular booth, Sam began describing what had happened over the past few weeks. Shortly after leaving the diner following our last meeting, he had reached the same point I had: he felt disillusioned and hopeless that he would ever figure out who he really was. He told us that it felt as though his entire reservoir of discontent had opened and poured over him, leaving him wet, dirty, and very unhappy.

"My relationship was falling apart, my sense of self was breaking apart, and the life I have worked so hard to achieve seemed empty." Sam paused for a moment. The despair he was describing was quite palpable.

"I was sitting in my car and everything seemed so hopeless." Just as he was about to continue, Lynn appeared at our table.

"Hi Sam, how are you? You look great!" she said with her characteristic warmth. Turning to Mary-Jane, Lynn held out her hand. "And this must be your wife. Welcome to Lynn's Diner."

"Yes, I'm Mary-Jane," Sam's wife introduced herself. "It's nice to meet you."

"Hi Lynn," Sam said. "Good to see you. I was just telling Ron the good news: I think I found the answer to my question."

"I knew you would, and this one will too." She looked at me with the infamous Lynn smile. "You boys are just too serious about all this not to succeed."

"Why don't you join us?" said Sam, and Mary-Jane nodded with enthusiasm. Sam's experience had obviously had an impact on Mary-Jane, too, and her gratefulness to Lynn and me was evident by the way she smiled at us. Lynn accepted and slid into the booth next to me.

"So what happened, Sam?" My jealousy had disappeared, but curiosity was getting the better of me.

"Well, like I was saying, I was sitting in my car a couple of weeks ago," continued Sam. "I was sitting there and sitting there and I was about to give up—not on life, but on this whole challenge of trying to figure out how to have a happy life and a happy relationship." He clasped Mary-Jane's hand, and she returned the squeeze.

"I sat there in complete despair. I told myself I was being ridiculous, since I have a great partner, a successful business, and all the money I'll ever need. But none of this mattered; I was truly upset. And that was the moment when I remembered something my mom said to me when I was young. I was just a boy, eight or nine years old. We were walking down a street by our house. I think we were going grocery shopping."

Sam took a breath. He was obviously still emotional about his revelation.

"Anyhow, we were walking down this street when we saw a homeless man sitting on the curb. He was older, maybe fifty-five. He asked for change, smelling of alcohol and obviously distraught.

"My mom was a good person, you know, very caring about other people and their struggles. My mom gave this man some money. I still remember being a little nervous about getting so close to him. I couldn't stop thinking about him for the rest of the day. Later, at dinner, I asked my mom why people are homeless, and I still remember how she looked at me. For a moment, it seemed as though her eyes contained the whole world's pain and suffering due to war or hunger or poverty or illness or lack of shelter. It was as though she recognized the pain in the world and was not afraid to face it."

Sam took another breath, choking back tears.

"I don't know how I understood all this, being just a young boy, but I could see in my mom's eyes that it was important to care about people and their challenges. Somehow, in that moment, I knew very clearly that I had the same love and caring in me that I was seeing in my mom. "

He paused again.

"In fact, she didn't say much in answer to my question. She said that we were lucky to have as much as we did, and that it was important to open our eyes to the fact that not everyone had so much. She also said it was impossible to eliminate all the problems in the world, but that it was possible to care. She said people were homeless because there was a lack of caring in the world."

Sam looked at us with tears in his eyes. "She died in a car accident less than a year later."

Glancing at Lynn, I could tell she was as touched as I was. There was silence around the table.

"When I was sitting there in my car, I remembered images I used to have as a child before this experience, and then in the years following my mom's death. Images of people all over the world reaching for food they had grown and entering schoolhouses they had built. Images of people who had suffered but who were now empowered, excited, and happy.

"I know it sounds naïve, but this became my mom's legacy to me. Helping those who need it most was a dream I harbored for years. But the task seemed so overwhelmingly difficult then. And then life happened and I forgot."

He sighed, and his voice grew stronger.

"But the thing is, no matter how naïve it was or that I forgot about it, it touched me to the core of who I was then, and it did so again when I was sitting in my car. When I look at my discontent more closely and think about my potential as a person, I now realize that caring about others is an important part of who I am. It's a part that has not had enough space and attention over these past years."

At first, I was astonished to hear old business Sam going on about the welfare of the world. And yet, the demeanor he had while talking suited him perfectly. His voice was clear and strong and he had a calm and powerful presence at the table. He was nothing like the tired and unhappy man who had sat across from me only a few months earlier.

I will never forget the moment when Sam shared his dream with us and I realized that all the hardness and fear, struggle and tiredness had fallen away from him, and a luminous person with a clear and resolute goal sat across from me. This was the Sam I cared to know. This was the Sam I most respected.

Mary-Jane turned to me. "Ron, I am so thankful that you started meeting with Sam. I don't know exactly what you both have done here, but it is partially because of you that Sam and I have another chance at happiness. Sam is alive and passionate about something again. And, to be honest, I'm excited about it too. We can't wait to start helping people that really need help. It's what we want the next stage of our lives to be all about."

Sam and Mary-Jane were beaming at me from across the table. I could see that this new idea had engulfed and fueled them both. In fact, it seemed that it was not only Sam's potential he had uncovered, but also an aspect of Mary-Jane's life and their potential as a couple.

"Sam," Lynn said as she got up to get back to work, "I am so happy for you. It looks to me like you have figured out an important part of who you really are."

I felt so happy and uneasy at the same time; happy that Sam had discovered something fundamentally important about his potential, but uneasy that I was still nowhere close to such a discovery myself. I tried to hide my negative thoughts from my friends, and soon became caught up in the good cheer that surrounded the rest of our lunch.

As we were preparing to leave the diner, Mary-Jane turned to me. "Thanks again, Ron," she said. "Sam was right to call you. The ideas you've talked about here have led to some pretty great results. Maybe you should write some of this down; it might make for an interesting read. After all, you guys aren't the only ones out there struggling with these issues."

* * *

When Sam and I met the following week, he still resonated with a sense of calm. It seemed as though a burden had been lifted off his shoulders, and all of his stress and anxiety had disappeared.

It was a sunny afternoon, the light shining in through the window by our booth. The diner was quiet. "So how was your week, Sam?" I asked, opening a conversational door for him to share more about his experience.

"Great," he replied. There was a new softness in his voice, a clear tone that spoke of the calm that surrounded him. "I am finally relaxed. All the pressure to act, to figure things out, to make decisions: it's all disappeared. I don't feel like I should be doing this or that anymore. I actually have a desire for something now."

He paused to gather his thoughts.

"Ron," he continued, "I'm happy with my life again. I enjoy everything so much more. Everything seems more fun. People seem friendlier. Mary-Jane is happy. The sun is brighter. Everything seems to be clicking. I know more about who I am. I feel calm and expansive. It's hard to describe. It's like I am part of something bigger, like I'm in tune with the whole world."

He beamed at me. "Remember when we first started talking about our discontent, and our potential?" he said. "At first I thought it was about figuring out what our professions should be, where we should live, that kind of thing.

"But when Lynn asked us the question—'who are you?'—and I went away and really thought about it for a while, I understood, for the first time, that it's not a question about how to live our lives. It's a question that homes in on this experience I'm having. I mean, look at my life. Nothing has changed."

Sam was right; his life situation was no different than it had been three weeks ago.

"Nothing has changed for me," he continued. "I have the same business and the same wife, and I have not done a thing to further the well-being of anyone else yet. And yet, everything has changed."

I had to disagree with him on at least one point; while he had not started to act on some kind of humanitarian project, he had already furthered my well-being just by discovering his potential. I felt inspired by his discovery. Somehow it seemed to encourage me to continue to push ahead in my attempt to figure out who I was. Sam continued.

"I haven't even started, but I feel different. My whole view of who I am and what life is and what the world is and how it all relates is different. I can see that I am an integral part of something beautiful, of something vast. I can see that I—we—don't exist in isolation. I can see that this feeling of calm and of happiness does not come from pursuing things that shore up my identity. It comes from dissolving it."

I thought for a minute or two while we each sipped our coffees. I was so happy to see him happy; it was an accomplishment we both shared. My discontent, however, persisted. "What about me then?" I asked, a tinge of desperation in my voice.

* * *

We talked for a while longer that day, but there was no movement on my own process of discovery. When I finally left the diner, I felt happy for Sam, but also a little defeated. It seemed that, once again, Sam had taken the prize in leaping ahead in his life while I remained struggling. But amidst all my disappointment, I couldn't stop thinking about Mary-Jane's comment. Her casual remark about writing down my ideas had sparked something in me. All my life, I had enjoyed listening to people's stories and helping them figure out ways to move forward. I had always been the quiet, pondering type, and there was nothing I liked better than thinking about why things were as they were. As a child, I had been an avid reader and I had always cared about knowing and understanding life. I had really enjoyed my meetings with Sam and the time I'd spent thinking about the challenge of making a real change in my life. But writing down my thoughts? I had never seen myself as a writer, much less an author qualified to espouse on a complex topic like managing personal change. But I could not stop thinking about Mary-Jane's idea of writing down what we had discovered during our meetings for the benefit of others.

The next meeting day came slowly, but at last it was time. When we met, I told Sam about the thoughts I had been having all week. Sam was encouraging.

"What if everything you've done in your life up until now has been right for you, Ron? What if all your interesting experiences and theories—about discontent, the unknown, finding your potential—are like a treasure chest of knowledge? Maybe this has been a big research project for you. Imagine that the research has come to an end. I mean wouldn't it make sense to follow Mary-Jane's advice and put it all down on paper?"

I still wasn't sure about it. I did not feel qualified and had never really tried my hand at writing, though I had read my fair share of all kinds of books. My uncertainty must have been evident on my face, because Sam reached over and gave me a gentle slap on the shoulder.

"You'll figure it out Ron," he said. "I mean, what is it you would really like to be doing? What is it that came out of the visioning exercise you did a couple of weeks back?"

The meaning of his questions came to me slowly, and then thoughts started rushing into my mind. In my visioning exercise I had imagined a more creative life, a life with more passion and much closer relationships. I thought of what Lynn had said to us, about considering not only ourselves, but what might most effectively serve myself and those around me at the same time. What potential did I have, not only as a single grain of sand, but beyond?

I'm not sure how long I sat there, contemplating my experience and my potential in the world. Finally, I looked up to see Sam staring at me, encouraging me with his expression. "What if this whole thing we have gone through—you and me, and Lynn, too," I started, "what if this whole process is something that can work again? Perhaps it could help others reach their potentials as well. There might be something here that could be helpful to someone else stuck in a rut. Maybe this wasn't just about us."

"I think you're right," said Sam. "You need to look at who you are, my friend. You have something to offer to yourself and to the world, something that lines up with everything else in your life. What you have to offer matters."

My mind was whirling. If I could help people discover their potentials, the positive changes they might make could even alter the world.

"Maybe Mary-Jane is right. Maybe I should write some of these ideas down." I looked up at Sam. He looked at me calmly and with a smile.

A wave of emotions washed over me. I had spent months—if not years—feeling discontent and trying to figure out what else to do with my life. Suddenly, everything seemed so clear: I had actually been exploring and realizing my potential all along. Unlike Sam, who had decided to make a significant change in his life and begin a new phase, my own situation called for continuation. I didn't need to start over; I needed to bring together what I had already done and begin to appreciate what I had already learned. I needed to put more value on the knowledge I had been accumulating and my abilities to listen and understand and create change. Instead of leaving these abilities behind, I needed to begin to embrace them. I was unsure how to proceed, but the same sense of happiness and calm I had seen in Sam was beginning to take hold of me at my roots. I had discovered the door to my potential at last.

As usual, Lynn's timing was impeccable. With another round of coffee refills, she slid into the booth next to me.

"You boys are good for business!" she said. "It's not often you see a couple of guys in here with such glows on their faces."

We all laughed. It was certainly a different atmosphere than had surrounded us when we had begun this process together.

Lynn continued. "Now you can finally start to think seriously about what you want to do with your lives."

POWER STEP THREE
Discover the Power of Your Potential

Within the discovery of a new aspect of your potential lies the foundation for taking effective action. Although both Sam and Ron are intrigued by taking a step that relates to helping others, this is not a prerequisite. You may discover a completely different aspect of your potential, such as the power to earn more money or to excel at a sport. You may discover your passion for an art form or for being a parent. Whatever it may be, use your discovery as the foundation for taking effective action to realize your potential.

I understood immediately where Lynn was coming from. I knew that, without having discovered these new aspects of our potentials, any actions we would have taken would not have resolved our discontent. Suddenly, it became clear to me. My dissatisfaction with my work did not come from the fact that I was in the wrong line of work or had studied the wrong topic. It was simply that my current job did not allow me to go as far as I could. I needed to break out of the box of being a business advisor and into the world of expressing my thoughts. Realizing this, my experience of calm and peace deepened. Suddenly it was clear to me what I had to do, and the urgency I had felt to make a drastic change in my life disappeared. Just then, Lynn said out loud what I was thinking.

"You don't need to make any radical changes in your lives to discover this experience, and you don't need to make any radical changes once you have discovered it. Just look at me: I'm still serving coffee at my diner!"

We all laughed.

"When you discover who you really are, your life and your experiences are somehow more calm and inspiring," Lynn continued. "And when new possibilities arise, you can be clear enough and focused enough and calm enough to recognize and realize them. For instance, new people may arrive in your lives, and you might finally be open enough to welcome them."

I suspected she was referring to Sam and me arriving in her life, but I kept quiet.

"From what I have seen, it's like your life begins to shine with a degree of strength, success, and possibility more powerful than ever before, and the actions you take are based on that same approach."

Once again, Lynn amazed me with her clarity. I was beginning to recognize the calmness and happiness she brought to our table every time Sam and I came to the diner. I was beginning to recognize it because I was beginning to experience it.

"Lynn, I want to thank you for sitting down with us that day," I said, feeling suddenly overwhelmed by everything that had happened that afternoon. "I don't know what made me suggest your diner for our meetings, but it seems like a miracle that I did."

Sam nodded in agreement.

"No need to thank me," said Lynn plainly, "it really has been my pleasure. And—speaking of miracles—coffee's on me, gentlemen." We laughed as she disappeared into the kitchen.

"What a gal," said Sam as we rose from our table.

"She really is," I replied as we departed. "I'll see you next week, my friend." We both knew that ahead of us lay the adventure of realizing our greatest possibilities.

THE THIRD POWER STEP:
Discover the Power of Your Potential

The process of discovering your potential occurs in relationship with your world. After all, without your world, your potential is impossible to realize, and realizing it would have no benefit.

Find a private, comfortable setting, and bring some paper and a pen or pencil. For the next few minutes, consider the most important parts of your world; for example, your family, your work, your neighbors, the environment where you live, etc. Note these things down.

Next, consider what you may have to offer to this world. What could you change in your life that might benefit you and your world at the same time? This could be anything, including a quality, such as humor; a career, say, becoming a chef; a hobby, such as mountaineering or pottery; or a particular way in which you want to enrich your relationships. Note down the most important ideas that cross your mind.

Now, review your list. Imagine what it would feel like if you took action and realized one or more of your ideas. Envision how you and your world might change as a result of your actions. How would you feel about yourself?

THE THIRD POWER STEP AT A GLANCE

STEP 3: Discover the Power of Your Potential

* Do not hesitate to involve a community of people in discovering your potential.

* Look at yourself to get to the doorstep of the unknown. Look at the world to discover your potential.

* To discover your potential, ask yourself: "Who am I?" and take into account the big picture when you answer.

* Don't copy what other people are doing to reach their potential. Everyone has a different way of getting there.

* Use the discovery of your potential as the foundation for the Fourth Power Step: Take Effective Action to Realize Your Potential.

FOUR

THE FOURTH POWER STEP:
Take Effective Action to Realize Your Potential

The following week, Sam and I returned to the diner fueled with excitement. We had cleared the biggest hurdle to resolving our discontent. Now it was time to act.

"How was your week?" asked Sam as we settled into our booth. I was looking over my shoulder for Lynn, but she was nowhere to be found.

"Exciting," I replied. "Very exciting." I had spent most of the week roaming through bookstores, searching for ideas and inspiration for my own writing plans.

"I can't stop thinking about the idea to write a book on this topic. It's such a great possibility for me. There isn't anything I would rather do and I'm quite excited about all the new places this whole exploration could take me."

Sam smiled, sharing in my enthusiasm. "That's great! I feel the same way. Right after we left here last week, I got started with my project. I've decided to create a foundation that will provide money to a variety of initiatives that fit my goals. I've already outlined a rough business plan, and have started looking into the financial and legal details. I met with my accountant to discuss tax issues and also had lunch with my lawyer to discuss the various legal ramifications I need to be aware of."

"That's terrific, Sam," I replied, excited for him. In his best Sam fashion, he had pushed ahead with passion. "What sort of initiatives would you get involved with?"

Just then, a waitress appeared to take our orders. "A couple of coffees, please," I said. Sam nodded. "By the way, where is Lynn today?"

"She's taking some time off," the waitress replied before moving to the other side of the diner to get the coffee pot.

"Taking some time off?" I looked at Sam. "Funny, she didn't say anything about that last week."

"I wonder what's going on?" responded Sam. Curious, we looked at each other for a moment before Sam continued.

"Anyway, to answer your question, I think I can raise some significant funds if I do it right. I want my foundation to have a significant impact. I'm going to see if I can create alliances with one or two of the big players in the international development arena. I did some research last week and have come up with a substantial list of possibilities."

I was impressed.

"How about you?" he continued. "What sort of approach will you be taking with your book?"

"Well, that's the interesting thing. When I looked through the bookstores, the books that attracted me most were in the management section—you know, books about effective ways to manage change and find new solutions. I realized that my background in change management consulting is a big part of what I can bring to this book. It would be a shame to throw away everything I've learned and studied over the years."

I felt a surge of pride. I had worked hard as a management consultant and had accumulated a good deal of knowledge. Now was my time to put it to use. And yet, even as I was explaining this to Sam, something seemed oddly missing. Although I had decided on a way forward that made a lot of sense, and despite the excitement I still felt about my decision, somehow the feeling I had discovered the previous week, the depth of experience I had touched upon, was already beginning to fade.

"I think that's a great idea," Sam encouraged me. I shrugged off any concern, determined to focus on my dream. "I kind of feel the same way," he continued. "You know, I've built up a certain set of skills in running and growing my business and I think those skills are worth something. It just makes the most sense to start from there. What I know best is money. So I figure if I am going to make my dream of helping people a reality, I need to start with what I know best."

We talked for a long time that day about how to realize our dreams. I explained the concepts I wanted to address in the book: managing transition processes, diffusing and differentiating roadblocks, strategically orienting goal-setting processes, and so on. I felt on fire with ideas I could include in my book. It would be a rich resource for anyone who was serious about learning how to manage change effectively.

Sam also painted a picture of what he was hoping to accomplish: his vision for how the world could and would improve as his foundation grew, the degree of influence he would gain through the new contacts he would make, and the spin-off opportunities that could result. He seemed to have an entire master plan in his mind.

"Can you believe this is happening, Sam?" I exclaimed. "To tell you the truth, it's making me dizzy just listening to you. Your ideas are so big. But I'm excited!"

"Me too, Ron. This is our chance to change our lives. This is our chance to shine. Let's do it."

Our conversation turned briefly to more ideas for how to realize our dreams; however, we were too energized to stay in the diner for long. This was the shortest meeting we had had at the diner so far. We had discovered our potentials and the confidence to turn them into reality. Our heads were filled with plans and solutions. We had found our footing to take action.

I talked to Sam numerous times during the week that followed. He called to run strategies by me, and I called him to discuss more ideas for my book. Things were beginning to take shape. During one of our many calls, Sam explained the progress he had made.

"I've thought of a great name for the foundation: S.A.M. It would stand for Shared Access to Money, but it would also stand for me, Sam. What do you think?"

I liked the name and told him so. We went over the more detailed plans he had developed for S.A.M., as well as the slew of action steps I'd developed for my book. My first step was to compile a two-page synopsis of my book concept and run it by a couple of my consulting colleagues. Sam's first step was to print business cards for S.A.M. and finalize the financial and legal structures for his new venture. The journey had begun. There was much to do, but we were motivated.

"Listen, Ron," Sam bellowed into the phone just as we were ending our call. "Earlier today I spoke to a business associate of mine, Howard. He's potentially interested in coming on board with S.A.M. I think things are really going to heat up for me here over the next couple of weeks, and it looks like I'll have to put in some serious time to pull this one off."

"Same for me, Sam, same for me," I answered. We were both on a roll and we needed to take advantage of the focus we had found.

"Howard told me he could dedicate some time over the next few weeks to help me get this off the ground. He's got a good business background and he would be a great addition to the foundation. So, if you don't mind, I thought we could take some time off from our meetings. It's time to go for it."

"Yeah, maybe not a bad idea," I replied. My feelings were a little hurt—I felt as though I had just been replaced by Howard—but I was too preoccupied with my own project to be too concerned.

"I'll call you in a few weeks and we can get together at Lynn's to catch up." With this directive, he hung up the phone. I felt slightly disappointed that our meetings at the diner were on hold. We had grown close again, and Lynn had begun to be part of our circle of exploration. I decided to call Lynn to let her know we wouldn't be back for a few weeks, but only got the answering machine at the diner. After leaving a message, I returned to daydreaming about my book.

In the days that followed, I received encouragement from the colleagues I'd contacted about the book concept. I even talked to Mary-Jane; I thought her background as an editor would be a great help on my project, and I asked for her feedback on what I had come up with so far.

I was making noticeable progress on the book, and yet, as time passed by, I found it increasingly difficult to focus. After a few more weeks, I was no longer even excited about the project. And then, one day, I was shocked to realize that the same old feelings of discontent were resurfacing. I was beginning to feel the same way about the book as I once had about my consulting work.

I wondered how this was possible. Had I directed myself into another prison? Where had I gone wrong? I needed to talk to Sam.

After a number of failed attempts, I finally managed to reach him. At first, he hummed and hawed about being too busy to meet, but—after being reminded that we had started this journey together and should finish it together—he finally agreed to meet me at Lynn's at the end of the week. He must have heard the tension in my voice and the concern I was feeling about losing the focus I had worked so hard to achieve. I felt terribly relieved.

The day of our meeting, I arrived at the diner a little early, secretly hoping that I would get a chance to chat with Lynn before Sam showed up. There was a lot on my mind and I was curious about what she would have to say. But Sam's car was already in the parking lot when I pulled up to the diner, and he and Lynn were already conversing when I scooted into the booth next to Sam.

Lynn spoke softly. "So where are you at, Sam?"

Sam replied with vigor. "Well, I'm basically set up. I've applied all of my business background, and I've developed a detailed plan for my foundation, S.A.M., which stands for Shared Access to Money." Sam was obviously still pleased with the cleverness of the name.

Lynn looked over at me; she appeared concerned. She turned back to Sam.

"So you named the foundation after yourself and you've used your business skills to set it up. Sounds reasonable. But I'm curious: how do you feel about it all?"

"I'm pumped about it," Sam responded. "I'm excited and I've been working hard at it." Lynn appeared even more concerned. "How come I'm not convinced?" she challenged.

Sam looked puzzled. "What do you mean? Besides, what does it matter if you're convinced or not? I'm well on my way. Didn't you hear what I've already accomplished?"

Lynn replied calmly, her voice even

POWER STEP FOUR
Take Effective Action to Realize Your Potential

It is easy to slip back into your old ways of doing things when you first venture out to realize your new-found possibilities. Reverting back to these old ways simply leads you back to your old identity and old feelings of discontent. The power of your greatest possibilities arises from joining your interest with the world around you. Focusing on actions that merely elevate your self-importance is a trapdoor into a new prison of discontent.

and clear. "You're right Sam. It doesn't matter what I think. In fact, it's really none of my business. But I'm not in the habit of hiding my true thoughts."

Sam slowed down a little and looked at Lynn. "Honest thoughts are fine with me, I guess," he said, though his voice sounded unsure.

Compassion and caring were visible in Lynn's eyes as she started to explain her feelings about Sam's plans.

"Do you remember when we last met, right here at this table? Do you remember the reason why you wanted to make your potential a reality?"

Sam nodded forcefully. "Sure I do. I wanted to help others. I wanted to make a difference."

"Well, not exactly, Sam. Not exactly."

I was beginning to be very interested in what Lynn was getting at. I suddenly suspected that Sam had faced the same difficulties as I had over the past few weeks.

"Sam, a few weeks ago, you explained that you were unhappy. It seemed like you thought you were dissatisfied because you really weren't living up to your full potential. You had not been aware of an important part of who you are, the part of you that cares and wants to make a difference. It's like it had been out of commission for some time. You had become too focused on yourself, and you weren't able to see the bigger picture. But remember, when you stepped beyond this limitation that day in your car, you experienced peace and fulfillment. Even without making any significant changes in your life, you experienced what it was like to live within the context of your true possibilities."

Sam looked perplexed. He had been so busy pursuing his plan to create a foundation that he had not really considered whether his pursuits were fulfilling his potential.

"What has happened to that feeling of peace and fulfillment?" Lynn pressed him. "What has happened to the feelings that led you to go after your dream in the first place?"

I was starting to understand what Lynn was driving at. Although Sam had discovered his dream, he had used his old identity to drive it forward.

"Sam, there is nothing wrong with using your business experience to get your project going. But your experience in business is only a set of skills. The true driver of your project needs to be that you care deeply about it. Imagine that you create your foundation using your old way of doing things—you know, your old identity. Assume you lose touch with the experience of peace and happiness you discovered when you were sitting in your car thinking about your mother. What kind of results do you think you will achieve?"

Sam nodded slowly, understanding starting to show on his face. "You mean I am using the very identity that caused my unhappiness? I am using that identity to create my dream? I suppose it could technically still work out and make sense, but it would be devoid of that experience I imagined."

"Yes, I think it would," continued Lynn. "But what do you think would be the result of that? I mean, if you create something anyway, why does it matter whether you live this experience or not?"

I couldn't restrain myself any longer. "I think I understand. It's going back to realizing that we need to move beyond being just a single grain of sand on the beach. It's remembering that our actions need to be based on our own interests as well as what the world around us requires. That's how we break out of the limitations of discontent. That's how we can accomplish something truly significant. That is how we can really stretch ourselves to

---

POWER STEP FOUR

Take Effective Action to Realize Your Potential

FIVE POWER STEPS TIP

To ensure your actions are effective, you can work to recall the feelings you had when you discovered your potential. Connecting your actions to the emotional experience you had when you discovered your potential ensures they will be aligned with creating your new identity.

embrace our greatest possibilities. It's so easy to forget that."

Sam began to nod. "This is amazing. It's like I completely forgot about everything that got me to this point and I charged ahead in the same old way."

"Yeah, it seems that way," said Lynn quietly.

An awkward moment followed. Sam and I had been so sure that we knew how to proceed. But now, our plans were being called into question.

"Hey, there's no need to get down on yourselves, boys." Lynn tried to lighten the mood at the table. "What you're trying to do isn't easy. It's like your old identities try to grab you and own you. It makes sense that you'd lose the experience for a little while."

Sam continued to look chagrined. "So perhaps I need to start again?"

"Well, you don't need to be quite so drastic. I mean, you've probably done lots of good things over the past few weeks. By the way, how are things going with Mary-Jane?"

At this, Sam looked even more crestfallen. "Interesting question. We had such a connection in Hawaii and it continued after our return. But over the last few weeks, things have started to slip back to the way they were before. You know, I got busy and we haven't been that close."

Lynn nodded. "That's exactly why you need to stay connected to the same feeling you had when you figured out what you wanted your life to be about."

Sam continued to look distressed. "But how are we supposed to do that? I mean, it seems so easy for the experience to slip away. I don't have time to sit around all day waiting for it to come back to me."

Lynn seemed to understand Sam's frustration. "There is a simple way to do this," she said.

This perked my interest. I had been falling into the same trap as Sam—perhaps even more so, since I had actually started to feel discontent again.

"The things holding you back and causing your discontent were the limitations you imposed on yourself," Lynn said. "Remember that. You have to go back into the unknown so you can get beyond those limitations and discover an effective way to proceed."

So far this was making sense. Sam and I listened intently.

"Sam, think of the story you told us about your mom, and how she carried compassion for the world in her heart and in her eyes. Think of the depth of her experience. Think of the power behind her words when she talked to you at dinner that night. To take effective action, you need to consider what the real opportunity is. It is so easy to get caught up in your old self. You know what I mean: naming the foundation, developing a business plan, making sure it all goes well. But what do these actions matter if you lose the depth of the experience your mom brought out in you?"

Sam stared at Lynn in silence. I think he knew that she was right.

"If you keep thinking about the possibilities that exist, not only for you but for everyone in your world, it'll be impossible to stay trapped in your limitations. Keep asking yourself: What will benefit everyone involved in the situation, including me? What is the opportunity that will benefit the bigger picture? Think about it for a minute," Lynn said, sliding out of the booth. "I'll be right back."

Sam nodded. He was visibly touched by what Lynn had said, and I felt the same way. We stirred our coffees in silence and thought about what we cared about. What were the real opportunities at hand? What was the bigger picture? What mattered in the larger context of our lives? Answers came to me quickly and forcefully.

"What are you thinking, Sam?" I asked, knowing he had also had an insight by the way he took a deep breath.

"Well," he answered, his voice clear and quiet, "this whole foundation idea is off the mark. It shouldn't be about me building another organization. The real opportunity is to continue my mom's legacy of daring to care. If I really let myself care, I feel a couple of things very strongly."

POWER STEP FOUR

Take Effective Action to Realize Your Potential

To reestablish an emotional connection with your newfound potential, step back from your situation and remind yourself of this question: What action will benefit everyone involved, including me? If you can discover what is beneficial for both you and the world around you, you have reached beyond your limited identity without foregoing your potential. Now you are operating from the point of view of the beach.

He looked at me directly and I recognized the same Sam who had shared his story about discovering his potential. I recognized the Sam who had made a commitment to fulfilling his potential.

"First, I feel that my relationship with Mary-Jane matters and that my business matters. I feel that my life matters as it is. I have an opportunity to care about my relationship and my employees and my customers. I have an opportunity to make a difference for people right now, and I am realizing how little of this I have really done. I mean, I have built something, but if I added a true sense of caring to it, who knows what good things might come?"

He looked thoughtfully at his coffee cup.

"And I am realizing how much I really care about Mary-Jane. I nearly went down the wrong path again."

I looked at Sam and nodded as he continued.

"And I think there are some other people I have not cared about enough. My sister, for one. In her own way, she's already living my mom's legacy. She is actively helping people around the world through her organization. Maybe I should call her to see if I can make a difference by supporting her organization, instead of building one of my own."

"Good idea," I nodded. Sam was back on track. "I think I may have been going down the wrong path as well. I mean, I took a step back and decided to write a book about management techniques. But is that what we have really been talking about? Or is there a bigger picture here?"

Sam nodded calmly. "What if you took Lynn's advice and thought about the real opportunity, the bigger picture?"

"The real opportunity, hmm..."

Like Sam, I took some time to think about the answer. I thought about everything Sam and I had discussed since we'd started meeting at the diner. I thought about Sam's mom, who had cared so personally about things far beyond her reach. I thought about Lynn's honest and respectful challenges about how far our potentials could reach.

Lynn shuffled back into the booth while I was still deep in thought. "I see you're thinking," she said. She looked straight at me. Her eyes were soft and her warmth captured me for a moment.

"I am," I nodded, "and things are becoming clear." I looked back at her and our eyes met with a clarity and openness I had not anticipated. I was momentarily distracted before regaining my train of thought.

"I don't need to write a book about management techniques. I don't need to base my potential on my past. I can base it on something else, something stronger. I can base it on what I know about, what I truly know."

"Do me a favor, Ron," Sam added. "Don't copy what anyone else has done. When I think about your situation, I see the potential for you to tell about what you know in your own way. A way that respects not who you were, but who you are when you realize your potential."

Lynn nodded. "I agree, Ron. This is a very special chance to be creative. This is a chance to figure out how to be you."

Late afternoon sunlight was shining through the diner's windows. The light reflected on the table and lit Lynn's face with a soft glow.

"I think you're both right," I replied. "I have to venture into unknown territory yet again before making any other decisions about how to move forward."

POWER STEP FOUR
Take Effective Action to Realize Your Potential

Each time you take action based on your emotional connection to your potential, you take a small step into the unknown. This is because each time you step forward, you take a small step away from your limited identity. Although taking even a small step can be scary, each time you do, you will be rewarded with positive feelings that come with a life lived based on your potential. Before long, you will be prepared to begin receiving the results of your efforts and enjoying your successes.

Lynn and Sam nodded. There was a brief silence around the table. It had been another emotional and draining afternoon.

"I don't know about you," I continued, "but I could use a few weeks to digest everything that we've said. I need to sort out how to move forward with this."

Sam nodded. "I agree. I could use some time to digest things too. And I also need to spend time with Mary-Jane."

"I'll see you boys in a few weeks then," said Lynn with a warm smile. We drifted out of the diner and into our cars. Once again, we were headed into the unknown to explore how to realize our potentials.

THE FOURTH POWER STEP:
Take Effective Action to Realize Your Potential

Taking effective action is not about making grand changes or achieving big goals. Rather, it is about taking a series of small steps into the unknown toward the realization of your greatest possibilities. As long as your actions are connected to your newly discovered potential, you will accumulate a significant and positive outcome over time.

To give this a try, take a few minutes in a private, comfortable setting and consider the aspect of your potential you are most passionate about. What is it you truly care about? What really matters to you? What lies at the heart of who you are? Consider one small step you could take today to move in the direction you consider to be most important for you and everyone else in your situation. For example, you could decide to phone an old friend or rearrange your closet or sort through some papers. You could decide to go for a run or make a deposit in your savings account or buy a new item of clothing. You could decide to take an afternoon to yourself or spend an extra hour with your kids. As long as the action occurs within the big picture and with an emotional connection to your potential, it will contribute to realizing your potential.

Write down the action step that will bring you closer to realizing your dream. Then consider if you are willing to take this step. If so, do it today.

THE FOURTH POWER STEP AT A GLANCE

STEP 4: Take Effective Action to Realize Your Potential

* Focusing on actions that merely elevate your self-importance is a trapdoor into a new prison of discontent .

* Connect your actions to the emotional experience you had when you discovered your potential.

* To reestablish this emotional connection, step back from your situation and ask yourself: "What action will benefit everyone involved, including me?"

* When taking action, keep the bigger picture in mind, even though the specific outcome may still be uncertain or the way there unclear.

* Be prepared to begin the Fifth Power Step: Receive the Results and Enjoy Your Successes.

FIVE

THE FIFTH POWER STEP:
Receive the Results and Enjoy Your Successes

Sam and I met again at Lynn's about six weeks later. It was a quiet afternoon and the diner was empty, except for a couple of regulars at the lunch counter. As I walked to our usual booth where Sam sat waiting for me, I spotted Lynn busily shuffling through a pile of papers and talking on the phone at the far end of the counter. A warm feeling of comfort flowed through me, knowing that Sam and Lynn were there to talk with me.

"If it isn't my two favorite customers," Lynn greeted us when she wandered over to our table. "Long time no see. It's good to have you back!" We were happy to see her as well. I had called earlier that week to tell her we would be coming back today. She had become an integral part of our journey, and she was beginning to become a friend as well.

"It's good to be back," answered Sam for both of us. Lynn fetched a fresh pot of coffee and three mugs, then slid into the booth next to me.

Looking around the table, I felt a sense of power and determination and clarity. So much had happened in the six months that had passed since we started our discussions. Sam and I were, without exaggeration, different people. I was proud of what we had accomplished.

"Boy, we have come quite a way," I said, and we smiled at each other. Knowing the intimate pains we had gone through to get to where we were only added to the sweet feeling of accomplishment.

"We sure have," agreed Sam. "There's a lot to catch up on!"

I nodded. I had spoken to Sam only a couple of times during the past few weeks, and not at all with Lynn. It was definitely time to catch up. Lynn opened the conversation.

"Well, how are things going, Ron?" she asked. "I've missed your friendly face in these parts." She gave me a warm smile and my heart softened. "Fill us in on how you're doing, will you?"

"Well, to tell you the truth, I haven't felt this good in a long time," I replied. "In fact, I don't think I've ever felt this good. I just never realized that when you open up to things beyond your limitations, when you step through the unknown and into what is really possible, the world looks so different. So many small things are happening in my life that I could never have predicted or even wished for. I wake up in the morning with energy and a feeling of looking forward to my day. I enjoy time by myself, you know, doing the small things like going for a walk, or sitting and reading a book. When I was thinking of making a change in my life six months ago I was so focused on my work that all I could think of was that I needed to find a new career. Now I realize that it was the enjoyment of life, the possibilities in my everyday life, that I was really missing. My career is still going through a change, and that feels good. But mostly, there is just so much richness and fun in my life now. It's kind of hard to explain. I just feel happy."

Sam and Lynn both nodded at me and smiled. I could see in their eyes that a part of their happiness had to do with seeing me relaxed and happy.

"The discontent I used to have has disappeared," I went on. "I feel like it was an experience in another life, another time. I mean things are even better at my job. Now that I know I will not be there forever, now that I realize that my real passion is for a life filled with these other experiences and thoughts, it just feels much less important and much less stressful. It's still a part of my life, but I know where I'm going from here. There is no rush anymore and that feels relaxing. I know that it's easy to get off track like we did before, and I believe discontent could even return with a vengeance, surrounding another topic, perhaps. But, if I can remain open to the expansiveness with which I am seeing the world now, I believe it will be difficult to get locked in again."

POWER STEP FIVE
Receive the Results and Enjoy Your Successes

FIVE POWER STEPS TIP

Sometimes you can get caught up in taking action after action to build your dream or reach your possibilities. Nothing is more effective in realizing what you have accomplished so far than taking the time to acknowledge your efforts and your successes. When you share your successes with others, you come to realize that, while there is more to be learned and experienced, you have already accomplished much.

Sam nodded in agreement, and he looked at me with pride and appreciation.

"Ron, when we first started—I remember it so clearly—you really wanted to help me. You were so committed to being there for me, and I don't know if I've told you how much I appreciated that. But quite early on, it became clear that you were in just as much trouble as I was. You weren't the hero you thought you were after all!"

I had to laugh at Sam's point of view. It was true.

"But you took the risk and stuck with me—and with yourself—and I will always be thankful to you for that. And look at you now: you're like a different man. So relaxed, so calm, so happy. And you're really onto something interesting with your book."

I smiled again. It was nice to feel appreciated for who I was and what I was capable of.

"As for me," he continued, "I couldn't agree more with Ron. I feel great about my life. Mary-Jane and I have found each other again. We have our ups and downs for sure—what relationship doesn't?—but we share a closeness and clarity now that just makes everything so beautiful between us. We're having a lot more fun than we have had in years."

This time Lynn and I smiled at Sam.

"My business is also doing well," continued Sam. "I'm actually enjoying it again, although my time in the office is now down to three days a week."

I applauded Sam. This was good news indeed!

"Ron, do you remember Robin? She's been with my business since the beginning. Recently, I realized how much responsibility she has taken on these past few years, and I finally decided to give her the opportunity she deserves. She's now my operational manager. I'll still work closely with her to manage the overall business strategy, but she's now looking after all the day-to-day aspects of the business. So far, it's working very well, and I'm happy to see her blossom. In fact, I feel happy supporting all the people in my company to realize their dreams in whatever small ways I can. It's like I now consider their potential and possibilities a lot more than before, knowing that if I can give them opportunities to step into the unknown, to face challenges that cause them to see themselves in different lights, then so much more is possible for them and our company. It has become a sort of passion of mine to support people in this way and it has made my days in the office really invigorating and engaging. It makes me come alive and I just love to see people step beyond themselves and realize that there is so much more they can do and experience, and there is so much more to life than what they had previously considered possible.

"These experiences we've gone through together are things that no one can take away from me. I'm proud and

---

POWER STEP FIVE
Receive the Results and Enjoy Your Successes

When you tell others about your successes, you help to solidify your achievements in your own mind and come to appreciate yourself more. But by reaching out to share your results and successes in an authentic way, much more than that is accomplished. By including others in your experience, you open the door for them to consider taking steps themselves and you may even come to identify other steps you wish to take yourself. Sharing your success actually creates more positive developments.

happy that I stuck with it, that I was honest with myself, and that I found my way through to this point. And I have some good new friends—though one of them is really an old friend—to boot!"

We laughed.

"But what about your dream of helping people, Sam? What's the status of it now?" I asked.

"Well, that's an interesting story. Not long after our last meeting, I called my sister Sarah. We had a long talk about all the things I had realized and about her work to help people—and about Mom. It was wonderful to reconnect with her."

Sam recalled their conversation with a smile.

"To my surprise, she called me back less than a week later. She had mentioned my interest in supporting her organization to the chair of one of their high-profile fundraising committees. She said that the chair wanted me to come spend a day with her and Sarah to see if development work would be my cup of tea. I flew out to New York a few weeks ago and spent the day with them. After I got back, I realized I had a lot of learning to do before I could ever become effective in this field. But I also thought perhaps one of the ideas behind my S.A.M. foundation—the idea to use my business skills and connections to raise some funds—wasn't so bad after all.

"To make a long story short, I called Sarah's colleague back and offered to volunteer on their fundraising committee. I now spend two days a week on it. It's very interesting work, and I'm doing some pretty high-level fundraising. It's a great experience to be part of such a committed group of people, and I know that my business skills are helpful. Even in these few weeks, I have really contributed to getting the financial side of their projects shored up, and the committee and Sarah's entire group are very appreciative."

I could envision Sam in his element, hobnobbing with other driven business entrepreneurs and getting them to participate in this philanthropic venture.

"I'm also involved in an outreach program with them," Sam continued. "We're taking our first trip overseas in a couple of months to visit a few of the projects the group is funding. Mary-Jane is coming too. We'll both be attending as guests only, but we still hope we can make a contribution. And who knows what will happen from there?

"Overall, it's been an amazing experience. It's really something I could never have mapped out for myself or planned on my own. It is beyond what I was considering possible in my life when I first faced my unhappiness a few months ago. And the funny thing is, Sarah has been asking me to get involved in something like this for years, but it didn't ever fit my schedule or my priorities. It took a long trip into discontent to point me to what I can really do in the world."

Sam was doing well indeed, and I was thrilled for him.

Lynn had been quiet all this time, but now she chimed in as well. "I'm so happy to hear you've both made it to the other side. It sure wasn't an easy crossing, but it seems it was worth every minute of the trip." She paused. "I have to say, these have been very special months for me. My diner has seldom seen guests like you!"

We laughed.

"Your commitment and your honesty have been heart-warming for me. It's great to witness people reaching new levels of happiness and success, it really is."

Lynn was right. Our accomplishments were worthy of being considered successes.

Lynn sighed. "Honestly, it has been wonderful to be part of this." I realized I had a lump in my throat. We had come to the good-bye part of our journey.

"I don't say this very often," continued Lynn, "but I've really come to like you guys."

Our booth was silent as we all choked back our emotions. It had been a pretty intense journey; I was both heartened and sad to see it come to an end.

"We couldn't have done it without you," Sam said to Lynn.

"Yeah, we couldn't have done it without you," I agreed.

"And isn't that what we've been talking about all along?" continued Lynn. "That we all extend beyond ourselves, that we are all a part of this expansive experience, that we are all in this big experience together? We *are* this experience. Good things can truly come when we realize this. I mean just look around this table."

We looked at each other and shared another quiet moment. The journey to explore our discontent and discover new aspects of our potentials hadn't been easy. In fact, it had been wrought with frustration and even more discontent almost all the way along. But, somewhere along the way, we had discovered a new foundation from which to explore and live our lives; it was this foundation that was the most important result of our search.

We were about to say our good-byes when the door of the diner swung open and Mary-Jane came in.

"I thought I might find you all here!" she said, sliding into the booth next to Sam. She gave him a quick kiss and turned to us. "How is everyone doing?"

"We're doing great," I said, as Mary-Jane placed a pile of paper onto the table. I recognized my manuscript. "We were just about to head out."

"Well, I'm sorry to interrupt," responded Mary-Jane, "but I wanted to give something back to you, Ron, and pass along some great news." She slid my manuscript across the table to me. "I believe this is yours."

Mary-Jane turned to Lynn. "Ron asked me to take a look at his manuscript a few weeks ago. This is actually the second version I've seen; the first one wasn't Ron

POWER STEP FIVE

Receive the Results and Enjoy Your Successes

Many of the results created by stepping beyond your limitations and engaging with your greatest possibilities are unexpected. They simply could not have been planned or accounted for before venturing out into the unknown. But even though they may appear to be unexpected, they are a direct result of your willingness to see yourself differently. Enjoy the unexpected results too. They would not have occurred without the work you have done along the way.

at all. Anyway, he wasn't sure about the new direction he was taking, and he wanted an outside opinion on it."

Mary-Jane turned to me, her eyes sparkling. "I really like it, Ron. I like how you've told the whole story—you know, the story of how these two old friends ended up reuniting in a diner, and how the owner of the diner started to become part of their meetings, and how they faced really difficult challenges as they tried to sort out their problems, and everything that has happened since."

Sam looked at me with a smile. "Does this mean you're admitting in the manuscript that you didn't really have a clue either?"

We all laughed.

"Yeah, I've told it pretty much exactly like it happened. And yes, I do say that I struggled at least as much as you did."

We laughed again.

"So you really liked it?" asked Lynn.

"I think it's great," replied Mary-Jane. "In fact, it's good enough that I actually passed it along to a potential publisher friend to look at. Well, she just called me a little while ago. That's why I decided to come by today. She liked it! In fact, she'll be taking it to her editorial board this week for consideration. Congratulations Ron."

I was stunned. When I'd given the manuscript to Mary-Jane, I had never imagined that she would pass it on to a publisher. I had certainly never expected that a recommendation would be made to have it considered for publication. I was baffled and excited.

"Mary-Jane, thank you! I don't know what to say."

Sam looked proudly at Mary-Jane. "That's great, honey," he said. "You're one heck of a friend."

Lynn and I smiled at Mary-Jane and Sam. Their renewed relationship was great to see. But a question burned in my chest. If I was to proceed with getting my book published, I needed to get Sam's and Lynn's permission first. After all, it was our collective story that I had written about. I was anxious to hear their thoughts.

"So what do you guys think?" I looked at Sam and Lynn and pointed to the manuscript on the table. "Is it all right with you if I share our story in this way?"

"Well," replied Lynn, "I would really like to read it, Ron; after all, I'm not sure what you've said about me. Who knows what a terrible character I might be in your story!"

We chuckled as she continued.

"Seriously, though, if you've made me even somewhat likeable, I think it would be an honor for you to tell our story. I really do. I appreciate the risks you guys have taken, and if your book can encourage other folks to take the same kind of risks...well, I'm all for it."

"I agree," said Sam. "Nothing would make me prouder than to have our journey together become encouragement for others. I think it's great, and you've got my full support—with the same caveat as Lynn, of course!"

We all laughed again.

"So did you write about everything we said?" Sam continued. "The time I had the realization in my car, my mom, everything?" he asked.

"Pretty much, Sam," I replied.

"Well, then you might as well add what we've been talking about today, too," he quipped. "Might as well make it worth everyone's while."

Everyone nodded in my direction, and happiness surged through me.

Lynn got up and returned quickly with her familiar coffee pot in hand. "So what about you, Lynn?" asked Sam as she refilled our mugs. "Will you continue to assault strangers in your diner with your random acts of wisdom, or do you have any other plans?"

We all burst out laughing at Sam's question. It was true. Lynn's way of prodding and poking us to move ahead in this process had been kind of an assault of wisdom. Our laughter had not yet subsided when Lynn answered.

"Well," she said, "as a matter of fact, I'm selling the diner."

The laughter stopped short. I couldn't believe what I had heard.

"You what?" Sam was astonished.

"I put the diner up for sale."

A few moments passed, then Sam started to laugh. "You're kidding, right?"

"No, I'm quite serious." Lynn smiled. "You should know by now that I don't mess around."

"But why did you put it up for sale?" I asked, astonished at the news as well.

"Well, I decided to sell this place the week after you guys first discovered your potentials, and you were starting to take action."

Something in my memory jogged. "Is that why you went away for a while? One of the waitresses told us you were taking some time off when we met here once."

She nodded. "Yup, that was when I decided nine years was enough. I called a friend of mine who is a real estate agent. She told me it would be next to impossible to sell this place, especially at the kind of handy profit I was hoping for. But I decided I wanted to do it anyhow. I have been running this diner for a long time, and I've done pretty well with it. I didn't really believe that nobody would want to buy it."

"And?" asked Mary-Jane. "How is it going?"

"Well, I've gotten only one offer from a couple who have just moved to town. They used to run a diner and they want to get into the business again. Apparently, they've been looking for a while, but they wanted something quite specific: a family place with a good long history, a good reputation in the community, and a solid base of customers. They wanted something with a bit of soul. It was love at first sight when they came down to see my place. They've offered me a price just below what I was asking. I have to make my decision by the end of the week."

"Will they change the diner's name?" I asked.

"I doubt it, at least not for now. What they liked about this place was the fact that it's a bit of an institution in the neighborhood. You have to admit, it's a pretty special place."

We couldn't disagree. We had witnessed the diner's magical powers.

"Wow," Sam sighed. "But what about you, Lynn? What will you do instead?"

"That remains to be seen," answered Lynn.

"But you must have some clue," I interjected. "There must be some ideas in that brilliant head of yours."

Lynn smiled at me. "Well, it's sort of a crazy idea, so I'm not sure I should share it yet."

We all protested at once. "If you're going to share it at all, this is the crowd to share it with." I smiled back at her. "We've been sharing all along. It's time for you to jump in too."

"All right," sighed Lynn, "here it is. Every week when you guys came in here, I got to thinking about how much I enjoyed our chats. I kept thinking about them at night, and I started to realize how much I like solving problems, and that I might be good at it. I think I added some fuel to your fire when you were stuck, right?"

Sam and I nodded our agreement.

"I thought so. I feel like, in some small way, I was a really important part of your journey. I suspect you both would have figured things out on your own eventually"—she nodded to Sam and me—"but I think maybe my two bits helped you to figure things out more quickly."

"You're right, Lynn," I replied. Sam nodded.

Lynn took a deep breath. "So I've been wondering: what would happen if I used this skill and applied it to other situations? You know, bigger problems."

"Bigger than ours?" I laughed.

"No offence, boys," replied Lynn, laughing as well, "but there are other, more important issues out there that need solving!"

"I agree, Lynn," Sam said, "but what exactly do you have in mind?"

"Well, I can think of a few different things. One idea I have is to go into business for myself again. I seem to have a knack for this; maybe I could do the same kind of thing I did for you, but with larger groups. Maybe I could even help companies sort out their challenges and discover their potentials."

There was a thoughtful silence around the table. I looked over at Lynn. Her hair shone in the light of the late afternoon and her face glowed with excitement. I hadn't realized, until this moment, what an attractive woman she was.

POWER STEP FIVE

Receive the Results and Enjoy Your Successes

Venturing out to discover your possibilities is an amazing and inspiring journey. Much of this journey requires a good deal of focus, courage, and determination. But no matter where you end up, discovering your possibilities means considering and reaching out into your world. While you are shaping your future and your life, don't forget that sharing the journey with friends and family is one of the greatest rewards of all.

"Lynn, I think you have a real gift for helping people figure out what direction to take," I acknowledged. "It's like you have the ability to see the big picture and how every little part fits in."

I considered my next words for a moment, not wanting to hurt Lynn's feelings.

"It would be a challenge, though. I think it would be a tough sell—you know, a diner owner being recognized as a credible business consultant. It's a pretty cut-throat industry, despite all its promises of teamwork and companionship. Still, you do have an ability to cut through the bull. If you applied yourself like we all know you can, amazing things could come from it."

Lynn looked at me, and I couldn't help but smile back at her. Her eyes sparkled with mischievous meaning. As I gazed at her, I realized how little I really knew about her. I knew she had faced her own mortality and made some changes in her life. But what other struggles had she encountered in her life? What had made her buy the diner in the first place? What was she truly hoping to achieve by selling it? Somewhere along the way on this journey there was something about her I had begun to appreciate a lot.

"You know," I continued. "If you're really serious about getting into the consulting world, I could put you in touch with some people who could answer any questions you may have. Or, if you'd rather, I can probably help you out. Who knows, maybe we could even team up."

"Thanks, Ron," she said, looking straight at me. "I appreciate it. I might just take you up on your offer."

She paused and continued to look at me.

"You know, I've really come to like you over these past few months. At first I thought you were a bit pompous with your attitude about knowing the way forward and all"—Sam laughed quietly—"but I have come to see what a caring person you are. You really care about your friends, even when they're struggling, and that is a quality not often found these days. I hope we can stay in touch."

"I would like that," I said. She was looking into my eyes and I was looking into hers.

"I would like that too," said Lynn.

Sam cleared his throat. "Do you figure it's time for us to go, Mary-Jane?" He pulled out a pen and scribbled a phone number on the back of one of his business cards. "Here Lynn, that's our home number. Call anytime. We should have you over for dinner sometime."

POWER STEP FIVE
Receive the Results and Enjoy Your Successes

Every process of change and growth comes to an end. But there is always more to be explored and discovered, and the adventure simply starts over. Another cycle of the Five Power Steps awaits. The end of one cycle is an important chance to celebrate your accomplishments and celebrate yourself. Doing so will give you the courage and inspiration to continue your life as an explorer.

Lynn took the card. "Sounds good," she said, "will do." She ripped the card into two pieces and scribbled her phone number on the other half. "And this is my number for you." Lynn passed the slip of paper to me. "You should call me soon."

I took the torn piece of business card and placed it in my wallet. "I will," I said. "I will."

Sam and Mary-Jane got up, and Lynn and I shuffled out of the booth as well.

"Take care, Sam," I said as I hugged him. "Take good care and stay in touch."

Sam nodded. "I will my friend. I will."

"And you too, Mary-Jane. Thanks again for helping me with my book."

Lynn and I waved at Sam and his wife as they walked out the door. I turned back to Lynn and, for a split second, I thought I might reach out and embrace her.

"Thanks for everything, Lynn."

She looked at me softly. "No need to thank me," said Lynn. "Just call me."

I walked to the door and, with a final quick turn and a wave, stepped out into the parking lot. I saw Lynn looking out of the window. I smiled and she smiled back. I don't know if it was her smile or the prospects that lay ahead of me, but I was elated. I felt like the whole world was open to me, as though I was one with it.

I honked at Lynn as I drove off, my heart filled with peace and passion. So much was possible. I had gone from being discontent in my life to pursuing what was most dear to me. I was writing and thinking and talking about the concepts I had cared about for so long. And then there was Lynn. When I looked at her figure disappearing in the diner's window, I wondered when we would see each other again. The sooner the better, I thought to myself. Had I touched upon the beginning of a whole new life?

Is this all there is? I had asked myself not too long ago, and I had to smile. At last, I thought to myself, at last you have answered the question.

THE FIFTH POWER STEP:
Receive Your Results and Enjoy Your Successes

Receiving the results of your exploration is an important part of the process. Consider the experiences and accomplishments you have achieved—even if you have just moved ahead a little—as a result of reading this book. Congratulate yourself on what you have accomplished! All accomplishments—large or small—are meaningful, and they provide the starting point for more interesting opportunities and explorations. Perhaps you have had a new insight about your situation or you have taken a small step already. Perhaps you have made a decision to inquire about your greatest possibilities, or perhaps you are considering whether an area of discontent in your current situation is worth exploring. All of these and more are accomplishments in and of themselves.

Take a few minutes to think what you could do today to celebrate your accomplishments. Perhaps you would like to begin sharing some of your thoughts and insights with someone else. Who would you like to celebrate your accomplishments with?

By completing this book, you have completed one cycle of the Five Power Steps. Go ahead and celebrate!

5

THE FIFTH POWER STEP AT A GLANCE

STEP 5: Receive the Results and Enjoy Your Successes

* Take time to acknowledge your efforts and your successes; this facilitates the completion of the process.

* Reach out to share your results and successes in an authentic way to create more positive developments.

* Enjoy the unexpected results too. They would not have occurred without the work you have done along the way.

* Realize that sharing the journey with friends and family is one of the greatest rewards of all.

* Celebrate your accomplishments and celebrate yourself.

CONCLUSION

What will happen to Lynn's Diner? Will Lynn's entry into the business world be successful? Will there be a romance between Lynn and Ron? Will Sam's dream of helping people become a reality? Stay tuned for more knowledge and tips on how to maneuver difficult transitions successfully when Lynn and her friends return to tackle even bigger challenges in the next book of this series.

As you've just seen in this story, there are five important steps to figuring out how to get to where you want to be. The Five Power Steps can be a powerful method for managing personal transitions. However, the ability to manage a transition is a widely applicable skill; the principles of the Five Power Steps can be used to solve business issues and larger social problems as well. The core message of the Five Power Steps process is that a negative emotion, such as discontent, can be a motivating and directive force for discovering a significant opportunity. Discontent should be viewed as a signpost that a change is needed.

In an idealistic view, positive change happens as a result of an inspiration or a dream. For example, a person might wake up one morning with a vision of how the world can be improved, and proceed to pursue this dream with vigor and energy until it is fulfilled. Unfortunately, this is a romantic, but not very realistic, notion for most of us. Most people (or organizations) are not able to dedicate themselves to greater causes amidst their daily struggles and responsibilities.

At the same time, the idea of the inspired hero with a vision is a narrow perception of the change process, because it is mainly focused on the self. In such a view, the individual is the source of all change, without consideration for the role of the world at large. And, while an individual heroic effort may be one way of successfully creating change, it is not how the majority of change processes arise.

Rather, change becomes a topic of interest for most people when some problem becomes significant enough to be considered intolerable. In other words, problems are actually starting points for change, in that they can help trigger the necessary commitment to explore alternatives to the status quo. As pointed out in Sam's and Ron's story, problems can escalate to conflicts, crises, and even destructive situations if left unaddressed.

The purpose of the First Power Step is to identify the source of this discontent. Once identified, it can be used as a lens to focus on the aspects of the status quo that need to change, and as a motivator to commit to the change process. As you saw in the story, Sam's and Ron's successful changes are achieved because they took the chance to share their discontent with each other. There is no real hero in this book. Sam and Ron and Lynn all contribute to the mutual discoveries of their potentials.

The Second Power Step requires a discontented party to realize that he or she cannot find solutions without first questioning his or her self-perceived identity—that is, his or her definition of "I." The way that the "I" sees itself is a limiting factor to the success of any change. The limitations of self-perception apply to companies as well.

In the story, Lynn's lack of formal education may have caused her to think herself unable to contribute to larger issues outside the world of her diner. At first, she may have considered her insights to be merely common knowledge, and not integral to Sam's and Ron's process of discovering their potentials. However, Lynn's self-perceptions change as the story progresses. She begins to see that the "I" she has been operating from could have something special to offer others far beyond her diner.

The Third Power Step coaches people to gain insights into their larger selves. The moment a person realizes a significant insight about his or her greater potential is the most important transformational moment of any change process.

For example, when Sam discovers that the desire to care for others is as fundamental to his nature as the desire to succeed, a whole new world opens up for him. As a result of his insight, his stance toward life changes, and he immediately notices improvements in his relationship and his attitude about life. In fact, he comments to Ron that, though nothing has changed in his life, everything has changed.

Insight allows for change, because insight creates the foundation for effective action, the Fourth Power Step. Any action that occurs before achieving and committing to the insight only prolongs or compounds the problem, because the action is derived from and reinforces a limited definition of self. For example, until Sam achieves and commits to the experience of caring as a fundamental aspect of who he is, his actions are ineffective. Sam's actions to build a charitable foundation—which were out of touch with his new insights—did not lead to any significant improvement.

Taking effective action is not about leaving behind the old identity and latching onto the new. It is about evolving it. In this spirit, rather than disrupt what he has worked to achieve, Sam finds a way to enhance it. True growth incorporates and transmutes one's old identity; it does not destroy or discard it.

Taking effective action is an art all of its own, and probably deserves more coverage than it has received in this story. There are numerous resources available that discuss and prescribe how to take effective action. But even if you follow the correct course of action for your specific situation, results will likely not be significant if you have not taken the time to work through the first three Power Steps. This is because many actions, while correct in their approach, do not occur at the right stage of the change process. The Fourth Power Step combines insight with effective action to achieve great results.

Acknowledging and celebrating success constitutes the final and Fifth Power Step. In the story, we saw that Ron did not know what the outcome of his exploration would be. After all, exploring the unknown is a key concept of the Five Power Steps process. The goals that Ron may have set for himself, or visions he may have had at the beginning of the process, likely do not reflect the answers he finds at the end. This is why the Fifth Power Step is crucial; to bring closure to the process, it is necessary to review, evaluate, understand, and appreciate the outcome of the process. Without completing the Fifth Power Step consciously and purposefully, you may actually miss some of the most important results. In Ron's case, if he hadn't sat down to discuss the outcomes of the process with Lynn and Sam, he may have missed what may be the biggest outcome of all: a chance to end his loneliness and find a meaningful relationship with Lynn or someone like her.

When facilitating business transformation meetings, I frequently conclude with a casual exercise that allows people to state positive experiences and views about each other. More often than not, this portion of the meeting creates the most energy and is remembered as a significant and important turning point in the business's success. Taking the time to acknowledge success and express gratitude solidifies the results achieved and creates a foundation for the next change process. After all, the Five Power Steps process is an ongoing cycle of growth and personal or organizational evolution.

Mastering the Five Power Steps cycle can be invaluable in these days of rapid change. Changes are afoot wherever we look, and the success of individuals, groups, and our world at large depends on our ability to enhance how we deal with change. This book attempts to help you not only embrace change as one of life's givens, but to understand how to achieve meaningful and significant outcomes of change. The Five Power Steps condense the most important aspects of creating meaningful change into a methodology that can be used in any situation for problems of any size.

There is a lot to know about creating an effective transition. All aspects of the story in this book are based on concepts developed in a decade of research and experience mentoring professionals and facilitating organizational transition processes. This particular story focused on a personal topic, but the Five Power Steps has also been used and can be applied in many business contexts.

If you have read this book, chances are that there is at least one situation in your life or work that you wish to change. I hope that reading this book has given you a sense of the results that are possible when you look at who you really are to inform what it is you should do. If this is the case, and if you have enjoyed this book and wish to apply the Five Power Steps further, I invite you to consider our series of self-study courses on the subject. These courses are intended to inspire and support you on the journey from discontent to fulfillment, an ongoing ride on which we all find ourselves as long as we care to grow. The courses provide additional background about each step, and are filled with useful examples and practical exercises designed to support you in mastering each stage of the process. You can find more details and registration information on our Web site: www.fivepowersteps.com.

I wish you the very best on your continued journey to your potential, and I hope you will find some good friends to share the process with you along the way.

All the best,

Andreas Abele

ACKNOWLEDGEMENTS

I would like to thank my editor, Lana Okerlund, for her creative support in making this book what it is, Natasha Zippan for her outstanding support and patience in creating the book cover and art direction, Christopher Moon for inspiring the initial seeds of thought that gave rise to a ten-year journey of creating and testing the Five Power Steps, Paul Geyer and Markus von Berg for supporting the realization of this project in invaluable ways, and everyone else who has supported the development of this project over the past ten years, including the external reviewers for this book. Most of all, I would like to thank my family for supporting me and being the heart of my life.

For more information about the Five Power Steps
and new educational opportunities, please visit us at:

www.fivepowersteps.com